Talking about Government

What is government? How does it work? It often seems very distant, out of touch with everyday life and ordinary people. Yet government affects every one of us in everything we do, as well as deciding the major issues concerning the country. But where does the power really lie? Do big business and the trade unions have too much influence? To answer these questions Eileen Bostock explains the system of national and local government in Britain today and compares it with other systems throughout the world. Using lively extracts from newspapers and magazines, the opinions of ordinary men and women and quotations from political experts, she reveals widely differing views on such vital topics as democracy, the use of the vote and the devolution of power. At a time when the future of government is under intense debate, this book gives a thorough and stimulating introduction to the subject.

Overleaf The Houses of Parliament.

Wayland Talking Points

Talking about Government

Eileen Bostock

"Elections and voting are our chance to show governments what we want or don't want; they let us have our say."

"Governments are by and for the rich, the privileged. It's not for, or by the people—as it should be in a democracy. The people come last in the Government's list of priorities." (Women interviewed by the editor.)

Wayland Publishers Limited

Wayland Talking Points Series

Talking about the Mass Media
Catherine Baker

Talking about Unions
Tom Brennan

Talking about School
Nicholas Peacey and
Jim Townsend

Talking about the Family
Russell Ash

Talking about Race
Russell Ash

Talking about Women
Eileen Bostock

Talking about the Consumer Society
Helen Turner

Talking about Drugs
John Wyatt

Talking about the Environment
Andrew MacKillop

Talking about Poverty
Anne Mountfield

Talking about Violence
Pat Ladly

Talking about Law and Order
Pat Ladly

Talking about Work and Leisure
Eileen Bostock

SBN 85340 269 8

First published in 1977 by Wayland (Publishers) Ltd
49 Lansdowne Place, Hove, East Sussex BN3 1HF

Made and Printed in Great Britain by
Garden City Press Limited
Letchworth, Hertfordshire

Contents

Introduction

What is government for?

People often think of government as being rather distant and removed from everyday life and ordinary people. But is it? What do governments actually do, and how do they concern us? Our security and defence is in our Government's hands, and the Government is responsible for our formal relations with other countries. But if you stop and think about it, government is really to do with every individual, as well as the country as a whole.

Look at the life of one ordinary person and see how important the Government is to him. His education, the house he lives in, the road or rail he uses to get to work, sometimes his job (if it is state aided or state owned), can all be provided by the Government. If he is unlucky enough to fall ill or lose his job, the Government makes provisions for him under the National Health Service, or pays him unemployment money. It tries to protect him against crime with a police force and prisons, and with a judicial system which upholds society's rules and punishes those who break them.

The Government also has to tax its citizens to pay for these services. Many of us grumble as wages and salaries are eaten into by taxes of various kinds and by ever-increasing prices. Yet it is all part of the Government trying to balance its books. On the one hand it has to look after society; on the other hand it has to charge society for the services it provides.

But government is not something that operates solely in advanced, industrialized countries like Britain, although inevitably the more complicated a society is, the more a government will have to do. Any society, however, whether it is big or small, needs rules to regulate and order the conduct and business of its people. These rules must be made and enforced by someone. If a society is to have a formal relationship with other countries and people, someone must be given the responsibility for this, as well as for the protection of the people. Where people want to live together, some order is needed for everyone's mutual benefit.

This does not mean that all governments are alike and that all countries have the same needs. This book will deal mainly with Britain, which has one of the oldest democratic systems in the world. Before seeing how it works, let's find out what a democratic system is.

It enables us to have a say in how our country is run. We can vote, in fairly frequent elections, for people to represent our interests and the area in which we live (the constituency) in Parliament. Furthermore, we can put pressure

Right Government provides education for most children at schools like this London on those in Westminster (the Government and our MPs) to do or not to do certain things. We can criticize and we can applaud the Government. There is a free press which can do the same thing. The press provides us with information about politics as well as voicing its own views. And, even if the party of our choice is not in power, it can often have a place, and a voice, in Parliament.

Not all of these things, of course, are perfect, but they are the kind of things that democracies rely on. The alternative — not having any say in the affairs of the nation and the way people are governed — has immense dangers. Could you trust one person, or one party, with the necessary power to run a country indefinitely? Would you like one body to do what it thought best, without any checks? Some people think it would be more efficient, others that it might not make much difference. Yet there is a saying that "power corrupts, and absolute power corrupts absolutely". Do you agree?

1. Find out what the Department of Environment deals with.

2. Should the Government be involved in all these areas? Are there any where (a) you would like to see it more involved, (b) where it wasn't involved at all?

3. Which do you think are the most important areas that government covers?

Chapter 1

How does our Government work?

Whether you like or dislike the political system under which you live, it is important to understand how it works. Through such an understanding you learn to influence events and take part in politics.

Our particular system of government is generally considered to be fairly democratic. For one thing, we can elect our representatives in Parliament; we can decide which party we would like to see in power and which policies we would like a government to carry out. Or can we? Who chooses the candidates we vote for? How often can we vote? Some say that once every five years isn't enough and that governments can do what they like between elections, without consulting public opinion. Others maintain that we don't really have a choice of party policies, because there are too few parties for us to choose from and the existing ones are all the same anyway. Further, it is argued that the smaller, minority parties don't have enough representation in Parliament compared to their support in the country at large.

Nevertheless, once we have elected a party to form a government, how does it govern us? What exactly goes on in Parliament? We all know that a lot of debating takes place and that laws are passed. But how are they passed? And how can oppositions make their views heard? Does the House of Lords serve any useful purpose at all, or is it just an élitist club? And what part in all of this does the Prime Minister play? He certainly is one of the most important figures in the House of Commons and has powers over and above an ordinary

MP. If he is so important, why do we need a monarch too? Many reject the idea of a monarch as being a waste of money. Yet in Britain the Queen has a useful role to play, although she does not have any real say in decision making. But who does? Officially, decisions about important policy matters are taken by the Cabinet, the Prime Minister's selection of the most senior ministers. Ministers, however, have been known to point out the power of the civil servants who advise them on all kinds of matters. And, before laws are passed,

consultation goes on between ministers and interested groups of all kinds, from trade unions to the Women's Institute.

Both before and after decisions are made, the media—television, radio and the press—can play an important role by informing the public what is going on. They also inform those in authority what they interpret as the public opinion of the day. Many people think that the media are too powerful. Others believe that the media should be free to watch and criticize.

All this is fine, but where does the individual come in? What can you and I do to influence government? Well, we could get involved in local government and either stand as, or elect, a local councillor, or, we could write to the press, or to MPs, or organize a pressure group of some kind. But do these things actually achieve anything? There are those who think that action of this kind gets you nowhere and that the only way to have any impact is to take direct—sometimes violent—action. All this, of course, assumes that you ought to, and indeed want to, take part in political life. Should you? Or should politics be left to governments?

Left Voting is one way of taking part in government

1 Is your vote any use?

Most people over eighteen can vote in elections in this country, but what good does it do them? Some people believe that voting is not really worth very much, that it doesn't give you enough say in decision making. Further, you can only use your vote once every four or five years, so what happens in the meantime? Others, however, attach great importance to voting, and maintain it gives people the power to choose, or get rid of, a government.

"A vote for a party means a vote for a government and for a programme. Each party is committed to a comprehensive set of policies, which range from economic and social matters to humanitarian questions. Foreign policy cannot be defined entirely in advance. Yet, as far as is practicable, each party describes the broad lines of its foreign policy to the electorate. Moreover, a vote is as much a judgment on past policies as on future action. At Westminster, in the press, and to a lesser extent on radio and television, the Government and the Opposition parties criticize each other and endeavour to show the consistency of their actions and of their proposals as well as the inconsistencies of their opponents'. Above all everything is done to emphasize the divisions between the parties. The electors are presented with alternate policies and, in most cases, should be aware of them." (Jean Blondel, *Voters, Parties and Leaders*.)

"I think you've got to vote. It was fought so hard for in the last century, you must use it. If everyone votes I think it has got a use. After all, elections and voting are our chances to show governments what we want or don't want; they let us have our say. If you don't use your vote then you can't complain about a government. We can either put politicians in power or remove them from it. But not to vote—to abstain—means you're opting out." (Retired woman, interviewed by editor.)

"Use? No bloody use at all. Look, how often can you vote? Once every four or five years. And what goes on in the interval? Voting makes no difference. One party's going to get in anyway and it doesn't make a scrap of difference which one it is. They're all the same when they're in office—out for their own good." (Office worker, talking to the editor.)

"I'd rather have a vote than not. At least if you can vote you're having some say in the running of things. If you didn't have a vote your life would be totally controlled by authority and they could do as they liked, without consulting you at all." (Housewife, interviewed by the editor.)

But what do people vote for? A party, an individual or a prime minister? The late Richard Crossman described, in a book called *Inside View*, what happened to him when he was campaigning during an election: "In 1945 I was new, and I was speaking earnestly through the loudspeaker as one often does. The windows, of course, one or two of them, were open, and there were two ladies I glimpsed listening behind the lace curtains. There was nobody else on that empty street except a very old man who was mowing his grass in his front garden, and he looked up at me and said, 'I wonder, boy, why you waste your time talking like that. You do realize, I suppose, that Coventry East would vote for the back end of a jackass, if it was labelled Labour?' . . . It's a humbling thought, for it reduces the sense of self-importance of any MP. It makes me realize that I was sent to Parliament because they want the party . . . not me. They are voting for the political machine which will

Right Cleaning the ballot boxes before an election.

BALLOT BOX
No
117
BALLOT BOX
No
129
133
BALLOT BOX
No
167
BALLOT BOX
No
178
BALLOT BOX
No
162
BALLOT BOX
No
33
BALLOT
No
63
BALLOT BOX
No
28
165

carry out the changes they've been promised. . . ."

The following quotes are from the *Observer* of 6th October, 1974, just before the General Election. Various people were asked how they would be voting. This is Michael Frayn, a writer: "Labour. Because whatever happens, one of the functions of government in a free society ought still to be the setting of some bounds to the tyranny of the fortunate."

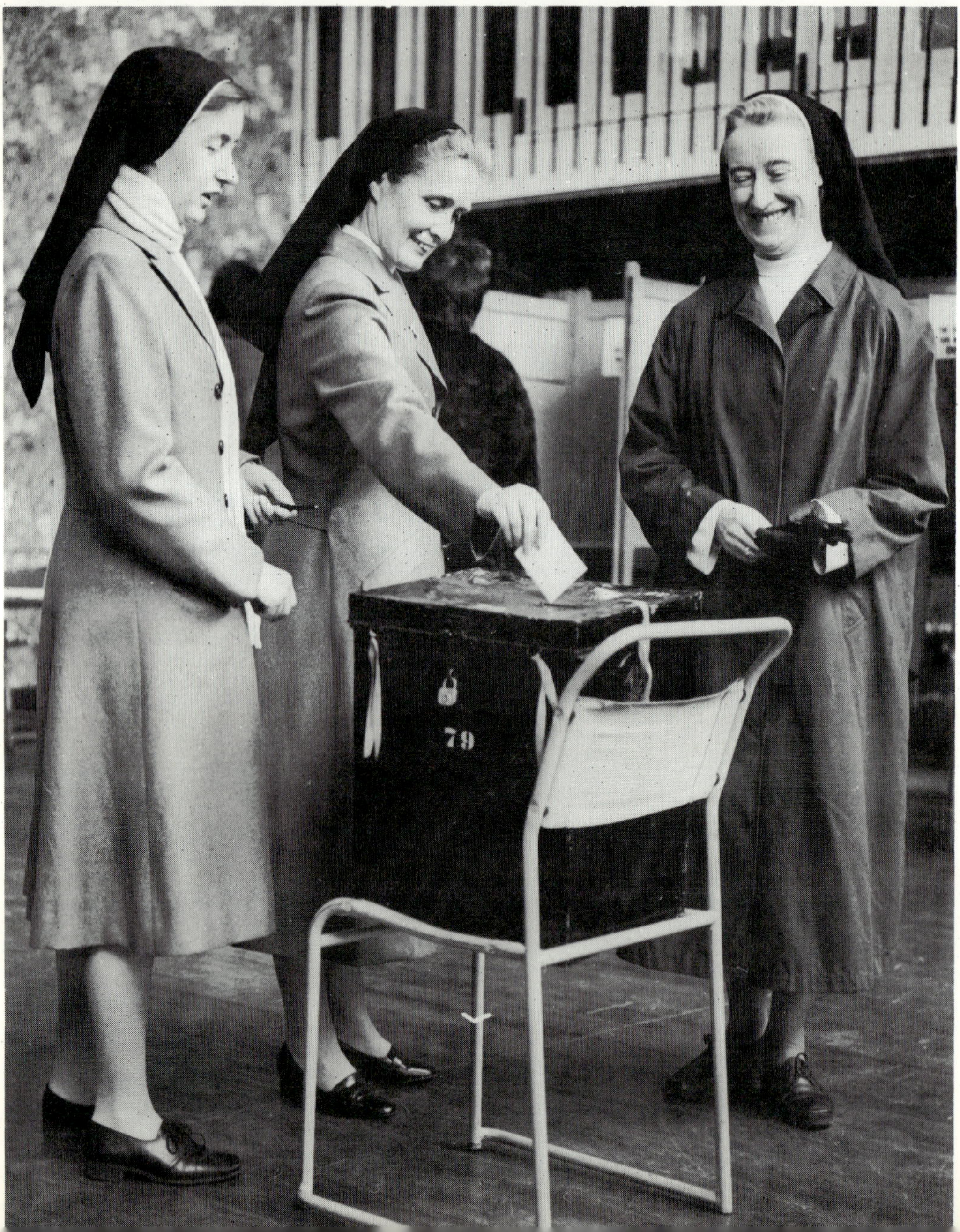

Colin Cowdrey, the cricketer: "At this time of crisis my vote goes to the team which I think will produce the best sort of country for my children to grow up in. I most trust the Conservative leaders to put the national interest first, to serve all the people and to preserve our heritage."

Muriel Spark, the novelist: "One can never hope for perfection in politics. But since, apparently, we made a mistake in electing a Conservative government, then made another mistake in electing a Labour government, I consider it foolish either to go back to the first mistake or to repeat the second mistake when there is a possibility of trying something else. And so I suggest that we try the Liberals."

Michael Holroyd, the biographer, said he wouldn't be voting: "I shall study what is said and written by the three parties; I shall weigh these millions of words exquisitely in the balance, then almost certainly do what I have done before: vote for no-one. I dislike our stage-managed political scene, which tempts on to the footlights precisely that type of person we least want there. Politics, I believe should be quieter, more factual, less newsworthy business. One way to bring this about might be by a massive dose of apathy, to which I expect energetically to contribute. Our economic salvation lies in the lost deposit. The only change you'll get by voting is more of the same."

Enoch Powell, the MP, told an audience in Birmingham that in an election the responsibility passed from the politicians to the people: "Very well, to be personal then—from *me* to you. It is your responsibility on Thursday to get what you want if you want it, to get what you supremely want if you supremely want it, or to be deceived, to be turned aside, and to get a parliament unworthy of you. Your next word is the last word." (*Guardian*, 25th February, 1974.)

Left Voters at the February 1974 General Election.

But does the British voter get what he wants? The electoral system is often criticized for *not* expressing the voter's wishes, (as can be seen in the section "What's wrong with our system of government?"): "The crazy, crazy British electoral system has performed its strange and unsatisfactory function all over again.

"It has enabled a party to form a government against the wishes of the majority of the voters. With the declaration of results [of the October 1974 election] almost completed, the situation showed that over 11 million people had supported Labour—two out of every five voters. Between them they elected just one more than half the total membership of the House of Commons. And another 15 million people supported Tories or Liberals—nearly three out of every five voters. They succeeded in electing 20 fewer MPs than the 11 million voters did." (*Evening Standard*, 11th October, 1974.)

1. Would you vote for a candidate for his own merits, for his party's policy, or because you thought his party's leader should be prime minister?

2. Do you think that voting should be compulsory, as it is in Australia?

3. Imagine you are (a) a canvasser for a political party. Describe how you would persuade someone that it was important to vote— irrespective of who you vote for. Now (b) imagine you are the person being interviewed by the canvasser. Set out your reasons for not wanting to vote.

4. Is the vote really "the people's power"?

2 How effective are parties?

The British party system is usually referred to as a two-party system. This is because the two largest parties, the Conservative and Labour parties, alternate in power, and the independent MPs and smaller parties can rarely offer themselves as viable alternatives in government. The system is praised by some for its effectiveness—the public is given a straight choice between two sets of party policies. It can decide which it prefers and which representatives it wants in Parliament. On the other hand, the system is criticized for discriminating against minorities and not accurately reflecting the wishes of all the people.

"I think there ought to be more parties—I mean I don't like any of the ones we've got, so I'm not really represented." (Woman talking to the editor.)

"I think you've got to have parties, haven't you? It's no good having a lot of different people not belonging to any party in Parliament. You'd never get anything decided or anything done. But I do think the parties could let their members in Parliament have a bit more freedom to vote as they like in debates." (Housewife, interviewed by the editor.)

The total support that parties demand for their policies can mean that independent-

Left Party policy is decided at annual conferences like this.

minded candidates don't have much chance of standing for Parliament: "At a general election, the electorate chooses between the respective party programmes. But electors appreciate the seriousness of their choice, and the floating voters [those not committed to supporting any given party] in particular are reluctant to vote for a party which is not united on important issues. . . . It is necessary, therefore, to have a programme supported by all candidates, and the task of ensuring that the nominee will support it falls to the constituency association. The views of each applicant short-listed are examined, chiefly to verify that they conform to the orthodox policies of the party. Generally speaking, constitutencies have little room for independent attitudes on party issues. Where the applicant is at all suspect, the central organization . . . may play a decisive part. . . . Even when elected, the member is still subject to some control through the constituency association. Not only must he account periodically for his stewardship, but the association is vitally concerned with its member's relationship with the parliamentary party. The essence of the party system is that a government can rely upon support in Parliament for fulfilling its election promises, while the Opposition can make a united attack upon these policies and present alternative proposals. This calls for loyal support in both debates and the division lobby [where MPs go to vote at the end of a debate], except where the issue does not involve party policy e.g. the abolition of capital punishment. . . . Otherwise, where he disagrees with his party, the most he can do is to abstain, and even this may be taken as evidence of disloyalty. The local constituency party has the last word. Where a member refuses to resign, he is simply not renominated at the next election." (Jack Harvey and L Bather, *The British Constitution*.)

Jean Blondel, a Frenchman who has written much about British politics, has this to say about our party system: "Political parties . . . are the main link between electors and their MPs. Without them, elections would be meaningless for the majority of voters who know very little about the candidates. Without them, elections would decide nothing. Parties are part and parcel of the real life of elections and of Parliament." (Jean Blondel, *Voters, Parties and Leaders*.)

Enoch Powell, MP, told an audience in Birmingham that politics and Parliament in Britain were about party, that without party there could be no responsible government, that electors vote not for a person but for a party, and not for a party in the abstract but for a party majority in the House of Commons. The elector was not at liberty, he said, ". . . to fashion . . . a party of his own—a bit from here, a bit from there—with none of the warts and all of the virtues, in order that he may have the luxury of voting for it." (Quoted in the *Guardian*.)

Is it true that electors only have a choice of Labour or Conservative? There are other parties, but with our electoral system most are unlikely ever to win enough votes to be represented in Parliament. (Again, see section on "What's wrong with our system of government?")

At the General Election of February 1974 several parties put up candidates. "In addition to the big battalions of the national parties, general elections bring into the field a multitude of small regiments, private armies and solitary freelances and samurais with axes to grind and hobby horses to ride.

"In 1970 there were fifty other parties in addition to the three main ones and the Scottish and Welsh Nationalists. These ranged from the Communists to such exotic and engaging militias as the Young Ideas

Party and the Vectis (Isle of Wight) Nationalists.

"The indications are that the field will be quite as large and colourful this time. . . .

"The International Marxist Group is fielding three candidates, including Mr Tariq Ali, the evergreen radical student and magnate of the Trotskyist Fourth International, who will contest the Sheffield constituency of Attercliffe.

"Mebyon Kernow, the Cornish Nationalist Party, is putting forward Dr James Whetter at Truro. In other constituencies it invites its supporters to ignore English party labels, 'which are irrelevant to Cornwall, and to judge the candidates as individuals on their desire and ability to serve Cornwall and its people'.

"Most conspicuous in the fluctuating band of one-man parties is Viscount Weymouth of Longleat, the heir to the Marquess of Bath, who is fighting Westbury in Wiltshire as a Wessex Regionalist. The Hardy campaigner wishes to abolish Parliament and divide Britain into seven self-governing regions answerable to the European Parliament in Strasbourg, and ultimately to a world government.

"The Workers Revolutionary Party has announced that it will be putting up nine candidates, including Vanessa Redgrave, who will contest Newham, North East." (Philip Howard in the *Times*, 4th February, 1974).

Edmund Ions suggests that there are dangers in having too many parties: "A multi-party system is fraught with difficulties of an even more dangerous kind. . . . For the ultimate horrors of coalition politics and minority governments, we might look at the Netherlands, where there are now more than 20 parties, 14 with representatives in the Lower House, and where it took six months to cobble together a coalition government after the General Election of November 1972." (article in the *Listener*, 1974.)

Dorothy Pickles points to the French system: "Of the many paradoxes presented by the French party system, the most obvious, and the most frequently commented on, is the picture that it conveys of instability, change and fluidity. . . . Between the two world wars, there were in the French Chamber of Deputies at one time or another, eight right-wing 'tendencies', that is opinion groups forming sometimes up to six officially-recognized parliamentary groups.

Both groups and names changed frequently. There were from one to four centre-right tendencies, similarly changing their labels and composition, from one to four centre-left tendencies, and from four to six left-wing groups. During the same period there were forty-one governments and twenty-two different prime ministers—twenty-three of the governments lasted less than six months." (*the Government and Politics of France*, Vol 1.)

Other systems operate in almost an opposite extreme, by having only one party. "On paper, the political system of the USSR, as detailed in the constitution, does not differ very much from that of a Western style parliamentary democracy. What makes it so different in practice is the fact that the system is worked by a single political party only and that that party is a highly-disciplined organization in which the leadership has a remarkable concentration of power. As a result all the important positions in the higher organs of state are held by those who also occupy prominent places in the Party hierachy, and this gives the various branches of the Soviet government a remarkable degree of single-mindedness and unity of purpose.

". . . The concentration of power within a single party is justified on the grounds that, as there is only one class in the Soviet Union, only one party, that of the working class, is necessary to safeguard its interest. There are over twelve million party members and candidate members. . . . Their task is to promote the ideals of communism and to foster loyalty to the state, efficiency in administration, productivity in industry, honesty and integrity in socialist enterprises, and a high moral standard of behaviour in all aspects of public and family life." (W H Parker, *The Russians*.)

1. Do you think there should be more parties in this country? If so, what could they represent and what might their policies be?

2. Would you prefer our party system, or the system of the USSR?

3. Do you think that there should be more independent MPs? Would you vote for one?

Left A by-election candidate discusses the local issues with constituents. But can any candidate or party exactly represent their views?

3 What goes on in Parliament?

Parliament's two Houses, the House of Lords and the House of Commons, have different functions and powers. The House of Lords is criticized by some because its members are not elected, but hold their seats because of a particular title which has been inherited or bestowed. Their political power is limited. Mainly they debate issues. They receive bills after the Commons has dealt with them. They cannot reject bills but they can delay them or revise them according to amendments suggested by either House. The Lords can also introduce legislation, both from the government of the day and from individual peers.

House of Commons

The House of Commons provides most of the action. It is here that major legislation is introduced, discussed and exposed to criticism and questioning. Here ministers and the Prime Minister give information on policy and are open to cross-examination by the Opposition.

Bills introduced in the House of Commons are of three kinds: public, private and private members' bills.

Public bills are designed to change the existing law and are concerned with national interests. Legislation can be introduced by the government to carry out election promises, and individual government departments can initiate bills on specific subjects.

Private bills concern particular interests, and are usually promoted by outside bodies or people. They confer special powers on local authorities, corporations, companies etc. For example, if a city corporation wanted to extend its boundaries it could introduce a private bill.

The procedure governing these two types of bills is outlined below.

Private members' bills are in fact public bills which are not introduced by members of the Government. Because of the amount of government business, about ten Fridays only are kept in each session for these bills, and MPs ballot for places. Many of the private members' bills are on important matters, which parties do not include in their manifestoes because they may be too controversial.

"The Abortion Act, homosexuality, law reform, divorce reform, the abolition of capital punishment—the mass public . . . was against all of them, and only the militants and special pressure groups were in favour. None of these reforms was in the party programme because of powerful objection groups. They were carried by private members' bills. . . ." (Richard Crossman, *Inside View*.)

How bills are passed

(Information taken from F J Wright, *The Study of Democratic Government*.)

Public bills

First reading—the title of the bill is read out by a minister in the House of Commons. The bill is then printed and studied by MPs.

Second reading—the principles of the bill are discussed, and a vote taken. This stage is regarded as the most important. Government bills are rarely defeated on second reading, but sometimes some of their provisions are altered.

Committee stage—ordinary public bills go to one of the standing committees. There are six standing committees for English affairs, each consisting of about twenty to fifty

Right The Speaker's Chair in the House of Commons.

Members of Parliament (including those who have a special interest in or knowledge of the bill's subject matter). The Scottish committee is made up of Scotsmen. Committees reflect the relative strength of the parties in the House.

Select committees are set up to report on particular matters, and very important bills are referred to the House of Commons as a whole—this is called the committee of the whole House. And who selects these committees? Not surprisingly, a committee of selection!

In committee, a bill is discussed clause by clause. Members are not so bound by party policy at this stage, either in speaking or voting on the issues.

Report stage—the bill is reported to the House and debated, if amendments have been made during the committee stage. Further amendments may be made, but this is not usual.

Third reading—the bill now has to be accepted or rejected as a whole. Only minor changes of wording are allowed.

House of Lords—the bill is sent to the House of Lords, where it goes through similar stages. If no amendments are made by the Lords, the bill goes for the Royal Assent (see Glossary). If the Lords make amendments, these have to be approved by the House of Commons. If the Lords reject the bill, there are procedures for settling differences between the Lords and the Commons. In any case the Lords cannot do more than delay legislation for a few months.

Private bills

The procedure for a private bill is different.

Above The Houses of Parliament.

First, notices about the bill's proposals must appear in the *London Gazette* and local newspapers; various government departments and offices are given printed copies of the bill; individuals who would be affected by the bill are notified in writing; and negotiations between interested parties take place. The procedure is then similar to that for public bills until the committee stage.

If a bill is not opposed, it goes for consideration to an unopposed bill committee consisting of five Members of Parliament, lawyers and the Speaker. If a bill is opposed, the proceedings take longer, and it goes to a select committee of four MPs called a private bill group. These committee members (appointed by the committee of selection) must be completely impartial. They assess the evidence presented for and against by lawyers. It is rather like a court hearing. The committee decides whether amendments are necessary and then reports to the House. After that, the procedure for public bills is followed.

A typical day in the House of Commons is described by Richard Rose in *Politics in England Today*: "The day may begin with a morning committee meeting. . . . At 2.30 p.m. the House assembles for prayers and, after procedural matters, departmental ministers answer parliamentary questions notified in advance by MPs of both parties; this continues until 3.30 p.m. At this point, ministers, opposition leaders, or backbenchers may raise exceptional or urgent items for brief discussion. For instance, the Prime Minister may make a statement concerning an international crisis, and answer a few questions about it. Usually by 3.45 p.m. the House is dealing with its customary business, discussing pending legislation or debating general policy questions. At 10 p.m. major debates normally end. The last half hour of each parliamentary day is reserved for an individual backbencher to air a grievance in an adjournment debate and receive a reply from a junior minister."

"The House . . . functions best when it debates political issues of some magnitude. Though it has also to do a good deal of committee work, politicians are usually elected . . . because they can make attractive and plausible speeches—though there are certainly many exceptions. What is more, these general political debates are the only part of the work of the House which receives adequate publicity. . . . The real purpose of parliamentary debate is to bring home to the electorate the major conflicts of policy." (Sir Ivor Jennings, *The Queen's Government*.)

"The first fifty minutes or so, upon every sitting day except Friday, is set aside for questions, usually addressed to Ministers. [The Prime Minister answers questions personally on Tuesdays and Thursdays.] . . . Any Member . . . can 'put down' a question, and may put down two oral questions a day. . . . Two clear days' notice must be given by the questioner. . . . When the Minister has answered, the Speaker usually allows Members to put 'supplementary' questions 'arising out of the reply'. . . . Questions, although ostensibly meant to elicit information, are also used for a variety of other purposes; to expose abuses, to ventilate grievances, to extract promises, to demand action, to embarrass the Government, and some of these purposes can be achieved only by a deft use of 'supplementary' questions." (Eric Taylor, *The House of Commons at Work*.)

The Government can therefore be watched and criticized by the Opposition in Parliament, but how much power do individual MPs have? Some maintain that party discipline is such that MPs follow the party line all the time. "The parliamentary party determines details of policy, agrees on tactics and disciplines members to ensure support for the party line. Membership signifies acceptance of its rules, the chief of which is to obey the Whip. . . .

"Maintaining day-to-day discipline within the party is the responsibility of the Chief Whip and his assistant Whips. . . . The Whip's chief function is to ensure unity of voice on policy and support from members when political action is necessary. Thus he communicates to backbenchers the line which leaders expect them to follow on a particular question, bringing pressure to bear on them to back it actively by their presence at the appropriate time. . . . Every week the Whip sends to the MPs of his party a notice giving order of business for the following week, underlined according to its importance, once, twice or three times." (*The British Constitution*.)

1. Would you rather your MP voted with his or her particular party in the House of Commons, according to his or her own conscience, or in line with the consensus in his or her constituency?

2. Find out who your MP is, his party and what his majority was at the last election.

3. Why is the Opposition so important in Parliament?

House of Lords

"Today the House of Lords has nc power over Bills dealing with taxation or expenditure, and it can only delay other legislation for a maximum of a year. Even this power of delay is to some extent illusory. The 12-month period would, in practice, be reduced to six to nine months because of the time legislation takes to go through Parliament. Nevertheless, some peers claim that the mere existence of powers (even if they are not used) has impact. A government, not wanting to risk being defeated (an embarrassing though not fatal event), will think twice before pursuing legislation it knows the Lords might reject.

"The Lords also point to their worth as a place where legislation, often drafted under great pressure of time, can be revised, tidied and made workable. Lord Brockway says: 'We greatly improved the 1971 Immigration Act.' It is true that on average 95% of Lords' amendments are accepted by the Commons, no matter what government is in power.

"But some feel the value of the Lords is overrated. Lady Wootton points out that the only 'second thoughts' on legislation allowed are those of the Government, and thinks the job could be done as well by having an extra stage in the Commons. Several observers believe that the work now done by many hundred peers could be done as effectively by employing more counsel [lawyers] on the drafting of bills in the first place.

"Opponents of the present House of Lords say there are two separate questions that should be put to the country. Does Britain need a Second Chamber? And, if it does, is the Lords the right one with its predominance of hereditary peers . . . and Conservatives. . . . The majority of peers believe a Second Chamber is vital. 'The

Right The Press Gallery of the House of Lords.

Below The British Prime Minister, James Callaghan, and US President Jimmy Carter at a London press conference in 1977.

sheer volume of modern legislation makes it impossible for one Chamber to handle it,' says one.

"They also believe the present House does a good job. 'For the time being', says Lord Boothby, 'the Lords, with all its anachronisms and all its faults, meets the acid test of any organization in this country: it works.'" (All extracts from the *Observer*.)

1. Do you think there should be a second chamber?

2. If so, should it be composed of peers or elected representatives?

3. Peers are not actually paid for their work, instead they receive travel and other tax-free expenses up to £13.50 a day. Should they be paid?

4 How powerful is the Prime Minister?

The Prime Minister is often said to be the most important and powerful political figure in Britain. He not only leads the majority party in Parliament, but also acts as the spokesman for the House of Commons. Government ministers and cabinets are chosen by him, honours and titles are recommended by him. It is the Prime Minister, rather than the Queen, who is seen as the political leader of the United Kingdom. But is he all-powerful, or are there limits on his power?

Above Sir Harold Wilson, Prime Minister from 1964-70 and 1974-76.

"Nowhere in the wide world does so great a substance cast so small a shadow; nowhere is there a man who has so much power, with so little to show for it in the way of formal title or prerogative." This was the view of William Gladstone, the Liberal Prime Minister of the 1880s.

Walter Bagehot, who in 1867 wrote a very important book on government called *The English Constitution*, said this about prime ministers: "There is nearly always some one man plainly selected by the voice of the predominant party in the predominant house of the legislature [the law-making body] to head that party, and consequently to rule the nation. We have in England an elective first magistrate as truly as the Americans have an elective first magistrate. The Queen is only at the head of the dignified part of the Constitution. The Prime Minister is at the head of the efficient part. . . ."

Richard Crossman, who served as a minister under Sir Harold Wilson, had personal experience of a prime minister's powers: "First of all, remember that each minister fighting in the Cabinet for his Department can be sacked by the Prime Minister any day. We must be constantly aware that our tenure of office depends on his personal decision . . . I am aware I am there at the Prime Minister's discretion. The Prime Minister can withdraw that discretion on any day he likes without stating a reason. . . . [Also] he decides the agenda of the Cabinet. Say that I think something is terribly important; I must get it through and I've had a row in the Cabinet committee. I register my dissent and ask for it to go to Cabinet. Somehow it does not occur on the agenda week after week. I fume—but the Prime Minister has the last word. The agenda is fixed in No 10 [Downing Street, home of the Prime Minister]. . . . He has almost a monopoly of patronage. He personally controls the Honours List. He has an unchallenged free hand in selecting new members of the House of Lords. Even more important than the control of patronage is the control of the Civil Service which a prime minister has exercised since the period of Lloyd George. . . . The Government's press relations are conducted by the No 10 press department at its daily press conferences. . . . It does not mean that he is a dictator; it does not mean he can tell his ministers what to do in their departments. But it does mean that in the battle of Whitehall this man in the centre, this chairman, without apparent power, can exert, when he is very successful, a dominating personal control. This is why a British Cabinet is always called a 'Wilson Cabinet' or a 'Macmillan Cabinet'. (*Inside View*.)

"It must always be remembered by prime ministers that they are not just answerable to their party, and to their Cabinet, but ultimately they are in their positions of power because an electorate put them there. That same electorate could equally well depose them.

"His departure might have been more moving if he [Edward Heath] had not outstayed his welcome. He left for the Palace to the sound of boos, cruel music to the sensitive ears of a man who had tried his best to serve his country.

"There he stood on the doorstep of No 10 smiling dazedly, blinking in the public eye for the first time since his dismissal by the people, misunderstanding and misunderstood.

" 'Misunderstanding and misunderstood', those words will do as epitaph for his premiership. For it was a failure of understanding on his part that was at the root of his inability to move the British people either, in his first abrasive phase, to 'stand on their own two feet' or, in his second managerial phase, to respond to the politics of pure reason." (Peter Jenkins, in the *Guardian*, 1974.)

Sir Harold Wilson, in *The Governance of Britain*, points to two factors that should constantly remind prime ministers that they are not omnipotent: "The Prime Minister and his Cabinet are accountable to Parliament. They survive as a government just as long—not a day longer—as they can count on the support of a majority of Parliament, however small that majority may be.

"The Prime Minister will, of course take part in the principal debates of the session. . . . But his continuing role in the House, the highlight of the daily Question Time, is his appearance from 3.15 to 3.30 p.m. on Tuesdays and Thursdays to answer 'Prime Minister's Questions'. . . .

"Prime ministers approached the bi-weekly ordeal by questions in different frames of mind, but of two things I am sure: no Prime Minister looks forward to 'PQs' with anything but apprehension. It has been said that Harold Macmillan, a highly successful performer at Question Time, used on occasion to be physically sick, or very near to it, before Questions on Tuesdays and Thursdays. In my address to the British Academy I said that, if Britain ever had a Prime Minister who did not fear Questions, our parliamentary democracy would be in danger. . . .

"The Prime Minister is leader of his party, not only in Parliament but in the country. Without the support of his party he is nothing. If he loses the support of the majority of his parliamentary party he is out. If he loses the support of his party in the country he is in danger. . . . If he loses the support of his party in the country, and cannot get it back, he should contemplate cultivating roses."

In America, this is not the case for the President: "If the Prime Minister requires only a simple majority to govern, only a simple majority vote is enough to bring him down. Not so with the President. He does not stand or fall on a vote in Congress. His party can be a minority in both houses, but it matters not. He is elected for a four-year term, and nothing can remove him except death, disability defined under the most rigid conditions, or the medieval instrument of impeachment." (Louis Heren, *The New American Commonwealth*.)

In France, the Prime Minister is in a different position, for he is chosen by the President and can be removed by the President—not by the electorate. "It is the President who, according to our Constitution, has to answer for the nation's destiny; it is the President who appoints the Prime Minister as well as the other members of the Government, and who has the power to change him, either because his task is accomplished or because the President no longer approves of him; it is the President who formulates the decisions made . . . promulgates the laws, negotiates and signs the treaties, ratifies—or refuses to ratify—the measures proposed to him, who is the head of the armies, who appoints to public office. . . . The President is obviously the only man to possess and to delegate the authority of the State. . . ." (General Charles de Gaulle, in a speech in 1964, when he was President of France.)

Right Edward Heath, Prime Minister from 1970-74, leaving 10 Downing Street on his way to hand in his resignation to the Queen.

1. Do you think British prime ministers are too powerful?

2. What do you think is the Prime Minister's most important power?

3. What do you think are the necessary qualities for a prime minister?

5 Do we need a monarchy?

While other nations, over the years, have got rid of their monarchs, Britain has successfully retained hers. Why is this? Is it because the British monarch has not tried to retain political power, but has instead allowed the politicians to govern? If this is so, why do we still keep our monarchy? What purpose does it serve? Many criticize the monarchy for the vast amounts of money it costs, and for its lack of political use. Others point to the non-political values in having a ruling monarch. What are these values?

Richard Rose, in his book *Politics in England Today*, quotes some views on the Royal Family:

"*Widow in Derby*: 'I hold with the Royal Family. You look to the head of the country. Keeps the country together, having royalty to look up to. They set such a good example.'

"*Leeds housewife*: 'You've got to have somebody at the head. It might as well be her [the Queen].'

"*Housewife in the Potteries*: 'I don't think there's any need for them. They are outdated and a waste of money. I have nothing against them personally.' "

In the same book Richard Rose outlines the role that the Queen plays in our constitution. "The reigning monarch . . . is almost exclusively concerned with dignified aspects of government. . . . The Queen must give her formal assent to laws passed by Parliament, but she may not state publicly her opinion about legislation. The Queen is also responsible for naming the Prime Minister, and dissolving Parliament before a general election. In these actions, the Queen is expected to act consistent with the will of Parliament, as communicated to her by leaders of the governing party of the day.

"The Queen receives major government papers, including reports of Cabinet meetings. She usually receives the Prime Minister once a week to discuss current affairs. The Monarch has the opportunity to encourage the Prime Minister, or to warn him about points that Cabinet deliberations have overlooked. No Prime Minister in modern times has suggested that he followed a policy because of the Monarch's wishes. The efficient as apart from the dignified responsibility for government remains with elected politicians.

"The institutional responsibilities of the Queen are necessary even if unimportant. In the absence of a hereditary monarch, England might have a president, like Germany or Italy, to commission each new government and to undertake ceremonial tasks.

"The ceremonial role of the Queen as head of state consumes a substantial portion of royal time. The Queen or other members of the Royal Family appear at a great range of public functions, from horse races and air shows to the laying of cornerstones for new local government buildings. The Royal Family is also in demand for goodwill tours overseas. Because these time-consuming tasks are performed by the Royal Family, leading elective politicians have more time for the efficient work of government."

Some schoolchildren on the BBC Radio Four programme *Fourth Dimension* gave their views on the monarchy to George House:

" 'The monarchy is a good thing—it brings money to the country with all the tourists'.

"'A lot of countries got rid of their monarchies and had a lot of trouble. Ours brings the Commonwealth together.'

"'I think we've gone too far now to get them out—we've had them rooted in our history for hundreds and hundreds of years.'

"'From birth we're conditioned to think of her [the Queen] as above everyone else—and it's only her money that makes her above everyone else.'

"'Everyone accepts the Queen as someone to look up to, and lead us.'

"'We're one of the few countries who've got a monarchy left and it makes us unique.'

Above The Queen opening Parliament. Is this just an outdated ceremony?

"'I'm sorry for the Queen—not allowed to mix with country and ordinary people.'

"'Do we need someone to be hounded by the media and held up to us as a model family?'

"'The press are always on at her, but it's us who's at fault, demanding to know all about her.'" (Schoolchildren from Walbottle County High School, Northumberland.)

There is a view that the monarchy is a safety valve preventing us from becoming too emotionally involved in politics. "It greatly stabilizes the system. Of course, we pay a price for monarchy; we can't get rid of the Establishment, the class structure. But in terms of siphoning off dangerous emotions, the monarchy has enormous value. . . . If [the Germans] had been allowed a constitutional monarchy, they might well have been able to prevent the coming of Hitler.

"It was because the Nazis were able to capture the emotions which are siphoned off into a monarchy, and to concentrate them against the regime, that they won." (Richard Crossman, *Inside View*.)

"The Queen received an almost embarrassingly warm welcome when she arrived in Auckland today for her fortnight's tour of New Zealand. Huge crowds made progress difficult when she and the Duke of Edinburgh went on a 'walkabout about the people' in, aptly enough, Queen Street this morning. . . .

"The *New Zealand Herald* remarked . . .

'People here overwhelmingly acknowledge the role of the Monarch . . . and in a world where so many heads of state must go about behind armour and under perpetual guard, what a thing it is that the Queen can walk freely among her New Zealand people with an absolute minimum of fuss and protection. . . .'

"After a civic luncheon, the Queen and Prince Philip met some of the 3,500 excited, suntanned children at the lovely Ellerslie racecourse, in Auckland suburbia. Back on board Britannia, they gave a press reception, dinner party and finally a larger reception." (*Times*, 23rd February, 1977.)

Other people are not so sure of the usefulness of the monarchy: "Now clearly, a society in which the apex of the social pyramid is hereditary, will offer less possibility of social mobility than any other. An American may dream of becoming President; a Russian, First Secretary; and a priest, Pope; but no Englishman can dream of becoming King. The monarchy thus acts, by its very existence, as a symbol, a manifest proof, that what you were born, you should remain. And though Englishmen and women have risen by their talents to the highest spheres, this potent national myth encourages the notion of our society being basically, by its very nature, hierarchically established." (Colin MacInnes, *The Monarchy and Its Future*.)

"What we live with today is a Cheshire cat monarchy, consisting of a bright smile surrounded by nothing, a frightened, timorous monarchy, hoping not to be noticed so that the death sentence may be delayed." (Geoffrey Bocca, *The Uneasy Heads*.)

Not all monarchies are like ours. By way of contrast let's look at Saudi Arabia, where King Faisal ruled until his death in 1975 in a very different way. He had absolute power over his kingdom, he ruled without a parliament and he held his own court to hear ordinary people's petitions.

"Every Thursday morning King Faisal bin Abdul Aziz sits in his green-roofed palace in Riyadh patiently listening to the grievances of the humble men of his desert kingdom.

"In the afternoon he may be talking to an Arab President, the French Foreign Minister or Dr Kissinger himself, pondering decisions which could influence the future of the Middle East and increasingly that of the Western world.

"Friday is the holy day, a time for prayer and temporal retribution. In the shadow of the great mosque in the centre of the city and before the eyes of a silent crowd, a thief will lose a hand or a murderer his head.

"Saturday, the beginning of the working week, is usually all twentieth-century bustle, encompassing perhaps the signing of a £200 million contract, the go-ahead for a massive petrochemical plant on a patch of virgin desert, the opening of a new girls' school and the delivery of a ground-to-air-missile defence system.

"As time ticks by in the king's palace, the oil revenues pump in at £1 million an hour.

"There are, in effect, two kings: Faisal, a subtle, experienced statesman with absolute power, and oil, huge unbelievable quantities of oil. Controlling the pace of change and upholding traditional Islamic values, while creating around them a modern industrialized society, is the main preoccupation of the Saudi Government." (*Observer*, 1974.)

1. Could we politically do without a monarchy? Could we emotionally do without one?

2. Why do you think so many people are interested in such events as the Silver Jubilee?

3. Should members of the Royal Family be treated differently from ordinary people?

4. What do you think is the Queen's most important function?

5. Do you think the monarchy in Britain keeps the class system in existence?

Left The Royal Family on tour in New Guinea. The tours are popular and save politicans' time.

6 How important is local government?

Local government, to many people, is far more relevant to everyday life than the activities of central government. It is the local council that is responsible for a whole range of amenities that are important for day-to-day living. The house you live in, the school you attend, the lights in your street and the emptying of the dustbins are the concern of local government. Why is it then that people in Britain are less interested in electing their local councillors than their MPs? Is local government in touch with the needs of the area it controls? Does it have real power to do things, or is it merely a puppet of Whitehall?

Local government has recently undergone changes, which we can briefly look at before seeing what people think of it.

County council elections are now held every four years, with the whole council retiring at each election. In the metropolitan districts, one third of the council is elected every year, except in county election years. County districts can decide whether to elect the whole council every three years, or one third each year except county election years.

Councillors are entitled to an allowance of up to £10 a day for time spent on council business. Each council fixes the daily rate within this maximum and a proportional rate for part of a day. The allowance is taxable. Councillors can also claim travel and subsistence expenses on a fixed scale.

There are four kinds of main local authority. In the six big conurbations the metropolitan county council is responsible for large scale structural planning, roads and traffic, refuse disposal, police and fire services, and the metropolitan district

Above Local government is responsible for fire services.

council is responsible for education, personal social services, youth employment, libraries, local plans and planning applications, housing, and environmental health.

In the shire counties, responsibility for education, personal social services, youth employment and libraries is with the county council, not the county district council.

Museums and art galleries, parks, playing fields and open spaces, swimming baths, and off-street car parking may be provided by any council.

Many district councils carry out work in the highways, planning, environmental health, libraries and other fields as agents of the county councils. Agency agreements can also work in the opposite direction.

Parish councils remain in shire county areas and have enhanced powers. Many of the smaller boroughs and urban districts which have lost their own authorities retain 'local' or 'town' councils with parish status. (Information taken from the *Guardian*.)

Just how helpful can the local council be if you have a problem? Supposing the street lighting in your road wasn't working, or somebody started building a wall right at the end of your garden blocking out any light you might be getting. Who do you go to? For most problems of this kind, and for any matter which is to do with the local area and its amenities, it is your elected councillor you must turn to. Sometimes he

Right Parks are laid out and maintained by local councils.

Left Home helps for the elderly are another local government service.

can be of help. A councillor in the London Borough of Hammersmith gave the editor examples of how he helped his constituents: "A married couple invited me round to look at an emergency fence the council had erected, having knocked down the adjoining building. The 'fence' consisted of coils of barbed wire and I thought for a moment that we were in Northern Ireland. A memo by the councillor (it was not me at the time) resulted in a more appropriate temporary fence being put up.

"A married couple living in a single room with poor facilities and several health risks, e.g. polythene round the cooker to stop the wallpaper getting marked (a fire risk). The wife (eight months pregnant and rather depressed and anxious) has to collect hot water from upstairs and bring it down to wash with. The owners of the house are a married couple and rent the room to the other couple for £6 a week and gas and electricity. They may have to get out when the baby comes. I wrote to the Housing Department to see what chances they have of getting somewhere soon. There isn't very much chance unless they are evicted when the child comes. I can, of course, stop them being evicted and also have the public health inspector insist on the house being properly appointed. But the couple have to live above the owners and don't want any more aggravation and unpleasantness. So they asked me not to take such

action. Hopefully I will be able to get them rehoused when the baby is born, or get them somewhere outside London. They got married thinking they would 'easily get a house.'"

Many councils and council officials do valuable work. "A council is starting courses in bricklaying, planning, and electrical installation for young couples who want to build their own homes but are unable to because of the mortgage famine.

"Cardiff City Council is also providing the land—and modest mortgages which cost no more than fair rent to repay. Each house will cost about £4,000."(*Guardian*, 1974.)

"Camden council is joining forces with the owners of a supermarket to help hard-up pensioners who want to buy food in small quantities.

"Under a scheme, which is due to be given final approval by the council's social services committee next month, the supermarket will sell on two half-days each week essential items like butter and cheese in smaller portions than are normally available.

"The council will provide transport to take pensioners to and from the supermarket.

"If the scheme is a success, the Labour-controlled council hopes to persuade other supermarkets to make similar arrangements for pensioners." (*Evening Standard,* 1974.)

Are all local authorities and councils as helpful as this?

"A slum in Salford, described by Engels in his *Condition of the Working Class in England* in 1844, is still standing, still inhabited, and in almost as bad a condition as it was in his day.

"Lower Broughton is a damp, low-lying district of Salford looking on to the River Irwell. Its cobbled streets are crammed with tiny two-up, two-down houses backing on to narrow alleyways. The houses have cracked and bulging brickwork, a few are demolished, a few derelict.

"The Salford Public Health Department declared them unfit in 1965 and in 1968 the council issued a clearance order and compulsorily purchased all the houses.

"Since then the council has allowed the houses to deteriorate further, often refusing to carry out the most basic repairs. There is no plan to demolish the dwellings and rehouse the residents for at least three years.

"Until a spotlight was thrown on the district in a recent television programme some of the houses didn't have lavatories. The residents had to use buckets and empty them down street drains. None of the houses has hot water or a bathroom, all have outside lavatories. . . .

"The bricking-up of unused houses has been so badly done that the rain comes in on the top floors and seeps into adjoining occupied houses. The streets are piled with rubbish, bed springs and rubble from semi-demolished walls, causing a multitude of serious hazards to children.

"In the last year Salford Council has built only 300 new homes. Its waiting-list, which has over 40,000 names on it, has been closed and no one on it is being housed since priority goes to people living in homes being demolished." (Report by Polly Toynbee in the *Observer*, 1974.)

Another criticism levelled at local government is that it is too easy for local government officials to be involved in corruption of various kinds.

"If a person is determined to make money by corrupt means local government will be his first choice. . . .

"In local government detailed decisions are made which can lead to personal enrichment, through planning consents, building contracts, and tenders. It is arguable, therefore, that the rules ought to be stricter here than in other fields. What would be a harmless social occasion in another context could in local government be a business lunch aimed at inducement." (*Guardian*)

Local ombudsmen, known as local commissioners, are appointed to handle complaints from the public against the main local authorities—the county and district councils and the water authorities. They investigate complaints of maladministration, normally passed on from local councillors.

Two Commissions for Local Administration—one for England and another for Wales—have been set up, and the national Ombudsman, Sir Idwal Pugh, is a member of both. (Information from the *Guardian*.)

1. Why is that, if local government is so important, only about 43 per cent of the electorate bother to vote at local elections? The turnout at general elections is sometimes as high as 75 per cent.

2. What would you do, if you were a local resident in Salford, to jog the council into some action?

3. Find out who your local councillor is, and whether your council is Labour, Conservative or Liberal.

Below Local government has to provide council housing and dustmen too.

7 Who influences government decisions?

When a government is elected it has the job of running a country and taking the day-to-day decisions about policy which affect all our lives. Who actually takes the decisions? Is it the Cabinet, the body that consists of the Prime Minister and the senior ministers he has chosen as cabinet ministers? Or do the higher-grade civil servants, those in the administrative grade whose job it is to provide ministers with information and advice on various problems and policies, take them? How much account has to be taken of powerful interest groups, such as industrial, business and trade union bodies, whose co-operation is essential for the success of a number of policies?

Anthony King, in his book *Why is Britain Becoming Harder to Govern?*, argues that governments are now in an impossible situation. They are held responsible for providing an ever-increasing amount of services, from roads, water and electricity, to sugar! Yet it has also become far more difficult to fulfil all these responsibilities, largely because any government is dependent on the co-operation of so many different people, and even countries. Hence the number of people who necessarily influence decisions could be said to be increasing too.

One example of such dependence on others was the miners' strike in 1974: ". . . [It] lasted for rather less than a month, though it had been preceded by an overtime ban lasting several weeks. Its effects were felt immediately. The country's industry was put on a 3-day week; there was a sharp fall in industrial production. . . . Politically, the effects of the strike were even more spectacular. It destroyed an essential element in the Heath Government's economic policy. . . . It lead directly . . . to the holding of a general election and to the Heath Government's downfall. Not only did the miners win, but their victory had far-reaching consequences for the conduct of economic policy by any future Government. By making it plain that, in the field of incomes policy, government had ceased to be the 'authoritative allocator of values for the society' and had become merely one participant, albeit a powerful one, in a complex process of bargaining, the miners' success effectively restricted the range of choices open to government."

He adds: "[It] seems probable that the state in Britain, and quite possibly in other Western countries, will . . . [become] merely one among a number of contenders for wealth, power and influence, the others including large companies, trade unions and their members, foreign companies, foreign governments, international organizations."

An ex-minister points to the influence of the administrative class of the Civil Service: "The power of the Civil Service is usually subtle, sometimes ruthless, but it is always there, like a great freemasonry—but more powerful.

"I just do not believe that the upper reaches of the Civil Service are disinterested in power. That is an illusion. Many senior civil servants visibly dislike the idea of a minister making up his own mind and rejecting their own advice." (Reginald Bevins, *The Greasy Pole*.)

"The decisions must be in the Cabinet. It is the Prime Minister's duty to ensure that any major questions of policy, particularly

Right top Confederation of British Industry officials at 10 Downing Street.

Below Trades Union Congress General Secretary Len Murray arriving at Number 11 to talk to the Chancellor of the Exchequer.

where there are inter-departmental questions, the possibility of inter-departmental disagreement, should be taken by the Cabinet itself." (Sir Harold Wilson in *The British Prime Minister*, ed Anthony King.)

". . . In the British system the Cabinet is the place of decision and the whole of Whitehall operates in terms of a continuous stream of written Cabinet decisions." (Richard Crossman, *Inside View*.)

After the February 1974 General Election, Harold Wilson (now Sir Harold) brought in some "outsiders" to help in decision making. A personal advisory team was set up to provide future alternative guidance on which to judge conflicting claims.

"And senior ministers will have at their elbows confidants whose task it is to judge issues in party political terms. They will also keep ministers in touch with grass-roots Labour feeling.

"Dr Donoughue's team [Dr Bernard Donoughue headed the team] are outsiders—mainly academics—aged between 28 and 40, but most have experience in Whitehall. . . .

"His men will be setting their minds to social, urban and economic policies, initially such matters as North Sea oil, land, trade unions and the social compact, and social welfare for all the less privileged. . . ." (*Observer*.)

Those involved in decision making in British government are many, as Jean Blondel points out in *Voters, Parties and Leaders*: "Informal advice . . . goes on, in many quarters, almost permanently. It is sometimes said that one has reached the stage when the administrators do not even think of a plan, of a suggestion, without having first to go through a lengthy procedure of consultation, submission of drafts to all concerned, reconsideration of the plans, resubmission of the drafts etc. For this to take place, administrators do not just listen to what committees have to say; they go out of their way to suggest meetings in Whitehall, they write and telephone to representatives of interests. They provoke advice from outside as much as they listen to grievances. . . ."

1. Who would you consult if you were a minister drawing up a bill on sex and race discrimination in education and employment?

2. How involved should ordinary people be in decision making?

3. Should government be dependent on different interests, or should it be able to take decisions on its own without consulting others?

Below The Cabinet in November, 1976.

8 The role of the media

Many people look at the media of a country—the newspapers, radio, television—to see whether that country is "democratic" or not. If there is a wide coverage of news, with criticism as well as information being provided, and no censorship of news or views, then it is assumed the country has a large amount of freedom. Just how important are the media in a democratic state? Are they too powerful, or not powerful enough?

"The liberal model of English politics demands a great flow of information between governors and governed. The greater the supply of information, the better informed the public and, as the public is expected to be the ultimate arbiter [judge] of policy, the better the policies of government. . . . Government is expected to supply information freely to the governed because the public has 'the right to know'." (Richard Rose, *Politics in England Today*.)

The press, radio and television all provide the public with news about the Government's and Opposition's activities and views, and especially at election times, they publicize the various party policies on important issues of the day. But another role of the media has been to uncover, and make public, information that they consider of vital importance to the public which has not been previously disclosed. Thus two reporters from the American newspaper the *Washington Post* discovered that the Democratic Party headquarters at the Watergate Hotel had been "bugged" by electronic devices and that members of President Nixon's staff were involved in this. The whole Watergate scandal was unearthed by the press. Its unravelling was both read about, and watched on television, by the American people.

Katharine Graham, chairman of the *Washington Post*, talks about the coverage of Watergate in the press. "Without a free and probing press, the events and import of Watergate would, in all probability never have been revealed. Without that same thorough, persistent, independent press, public debate could not proceed, and the clamour and clash of opinions might never be distilled into that 'deliberate sense of the community' which decides the matter in the end. . . .

"The great American experiment is at a perilous, inconclusive point. If any lesson has emerged from the turmoil and tragedy so far, it is that the press in America should be more free, not less. More vigorous and probing. More alert to its large responsibilities—and less easily satisfied with its own performance.

"[It is] the essential function of the American press—to probe, to ask inconvenient questions, to report fully and fairly what is going on, and thus to keep the Government accountable. It is an adversary system, often more heated and contentious than we might like. And it is less efficient than it ought to be. But it's a necessary job." (Terry Coleman interviewing Katharine Graham in the *Guardian*.)

In contrast, the press in the Lebanon is far from free:

"No direct references to the fighting appear in the local press, which is subject to government censorship. . . .

"President Sarkis did wisely decide to put a stop to the censorship of foreign correspondents, who can now report with complete freedom on the war's aftermath, the battles in southern Lebanon and the task of reconstruction in Beirut. But when foreign magazines and newspapers go on

Right top Carl Bernstein (left) and Bob Woodward (right), the *Washington Post* reporters who uncovered the Watergate scandal.

Below Former US President Richard Nixon. Was he "sold" to the voters in television commercials?

sale in Beirut, the censors have already been to work with their scissors, cutting out articles which the rest of the world can read but which the Lebanese may not." (The *Times*, 3rd May, 1977.)

Yet although the British press is commonly regarded as being fairly free from interference by government, just how independent is it?

One of the strictest limitations is the D-notice system. This is the Government's unofficial way of letting the press know what it can and cannot publish for security reasons. A committee, comprising defence ministers and representatives from the press and broadcasting, as well as Service members, was originally set up in 1912 for this purpose, and although it has no legal basis it still exists today. "The aim of the arrangements is to make clear to the press what the Government is willing that it should publish on security matters and what it does not wish it to publish. The press and broadcasting bodies have the unofficial assurance that they will not be prosecuted under the Official Secrets Acts so long as they comply; the Government expects to prevent the disclosure of technical and strategic information. . . . The lists of permitted and forbidden matter are circulated in D-notices to the publications likely to be concerned." (H Street, *Freedom, the Individual and the Law*.)

"[In 1967] Chapman Pincher, the *Express*'s defence correspondent, with many scoops gracing his personal cuttings file, learned that every night all overseas cables sent that day were collected from the offices of the cable companies and taken to the Ministry of Defence for vetting. He checked with Colonel Lohan [then secretary of the D-notice committee] and was told or was given the impression, that no D-notice applied to the story. So the *Express* decided to print it. . . .

"Next day in the Commons, Prime Minister Harold Wilson condemned the paper for publishing. It was a breach of two D-notices, he said, which it wasn't, and the *Express* had been repeatedly warned, he added, which it hadn't. A Privy Councillors' Commission completely exonerated the *Express*, but the Government indicated its displeasure by issuing a White Paper which simply disagreed with the Privy Councillors. In a Lords debate, Lord Radcliffe came out with what really ought to be the last words on the subject: 'Governments always tend to want not a really free press, but a well-managed or well-conducted press. . . . They have all the resources of modern public relations at their beck and call. They have all the subtle acts of pressure, the nods and winks, the smile at what is called the responsible reporter, and the frown at the man who does not see quite clearly the Government's point of view. There is nothing evil about this. But it is one of the conflicts that goes on between government—whatever government it is—and the press who are seeking to do their duty of telling the public the news. The Government have all these resources to play on—and they have the Official Secrets Act.'" (Bill Grundy, *The Press Inside Out*.)

In a BBC 2 television programme, "What do you think of it so far?", different views were discussed on the impact television had on the public.

Geoffrey Johnson Smith, a Conservative MP, was asked if he thought that television had ever affected the result of an election in Britain. He replied: "I don't think it has affected the result of an election. Lord help us, what sort of a democracy would it be if the result of an election were affected by television? But it has some effect, I am sure it

Right Paratroopers chasing rioters in Northern Ireland. Can the media cover events in Ulster objectively?

does. I think it helps to make people better informed. Between elections, it can help create the image, or sustain an image, of a party. Once the politicians start getting down to too much detail about policies, well, they bore the pants off them on television, because it is still regarded as a vehicle of entertainment."

Jonathan Dimbleby, a television reporter, complained that so many restraints were put on television reporters in an attempt to keep reporting "objective" that it was very difficult for reporters to report matters "honestly".

". . . There has not been on British television since 1968, a serious, detailed account of the history of Northern Ireland. And that is because it is a very delicate, politically sensitive issue which is very difficult to do adequately on television, and therefore the job has been baulked. It should not be baulked, and the reason why it is baulked is because of the political institutions: BBC, IBA, British Government, British Opposition, who don't wish us to know too much too well about Northern Ireland." (Reported in the *Listener*, 9th September, 1976.)

It has been argued by some that television has become too commercialized, that it has reduced politicians to the level of commercial products. People are packaged and sold in much the same way as any other item that is advertised through the medium of television. Criticism of this sort has been levelled particularly at television in the United States of America. Joe McGinniss, in his book *The Selling of the President*, describes how people were employed

specifically to sell Richard Nixon to the public through television. The technique is similar to that used by an advertising agency.

"[People's] *response is to the image, not to the man*. . . . It's not what's *there* that counts, it's what's projected. . . . Politics is much more emotional than it is rational, and this is particularly true of presidential politics. People identify with a president in a way they do with no other public figure. Potential presidents are measured against an ideal that's a combination of leading man, God, father, hero, pope, king, with maybe just a touch of the avenging Furies thrown in. They want him to be larger than life, a living legend, and yet quintessentially human; someone to be held up to their children as a model. . . . Selection of a president has to be an act of faith. It becomes increasingly so as the business of government becomes ever more incomprehensible to the average voter. This faith isn't achieved by reason; it's achieved by charisma, by a *feeling* of trust that can't be argued or reasoned. . . .

"[This] suggests that we take the time and the money to experiment, in a controlled manner, with film and television techniques, with . . . uses of the television medium that can *best* convey the *image* we want to get across."

But the media can often ignore the desired image. Cartoons, satirical magazines, television mimics and comedians are free to make us laugh at those in power:

"Last year a Cabinet Minister had everyone snoring and yawning for hours while he stood in a stricken field somewhere in East Anglia holding up a tiny, shrivelled potato. . . .

"That was supposed to show the Government's AWARENESS OF THE GRAVITY OF THE SITUATION, deep CONCERN for the

problems of the farmer and what high potato prices would do to the cost of the HOUSE-WIFE'S SHOPPING BAG.

"Will non-drought stop Cabinet Ministers putting on that sort of act? It will not.

"One of them will go and stand in a fertile field, the same field somewhere in East Anglia, and hold up a potato the size of his head.

"This will show that despite snide criticism and doom-saying, things are going well, and the farmer and the housewife should be grateful and support a policy which etc. etc. until North Sea oil turns the corner and flows like manna towards a golden future." (*Private Eye*, 1977.)

"The Pope may launch his
Interdict,
The Union its decree,
But the bubble is blown and
the bubble is pricked
By Us and such as We.
Remember the battle and
stand aside
While Thrones and
Powers confess
That King over all the chil-
dren of pride
Is the Press—the Press—
the Press!"
(Rudyard Kipling, *The Press*.)

1. Geoffrey Johnson Smith said that people are bored by too much detail about policies. Do you think this is true, or is it that the authorities don't want us to know too many details?

2. Do you think Parliament should be televised?

3. Should the media have more or less power?

4. Why is the Press" King over all the children of pride"?

9 How can you influence government?

The power of numbers in politics is generally considered to be more effective than the actions of the individual. Is it true that "the threat of the many is greater than the threat of one"? How can groups influence those in power more efficiently than one person? What sort of actions can people, collectively or singly, take to exert pressure on those in authority? Does it mean the individual is powerless in politics? Does authority listen to people's pleas anyway?

As an individual you can either write to your MP with a complaint or request, or you can "lobby" him—by yourself or with others. Lobbying your MP means that you go along to the House of Commons and fill in a form, in the lobby of the House, requesting a meeting with your MP. On the form you put your name, your constituency and the reason why you want to see him. One of the officials of the House then goes in search of the appropriate MP and, if he is to be found, you can then discuss your problem with him. Anyone can do this, and the practice is regarded as a right of every citizen in a democracy. Do MPs pay any attention to your letters and lobbying?

Lord Winstanley said that when he was a Liberal MP he spent "fifty hours a week dealing with correspondence." He went on, "I can help my constituents. I've just got compensation for a woman who lost a parcel in the post office. A woman in my constituency is Spanish and her husband couldn't get a permit to live here. I managed to change that. You see the individual Member of Parliament has no power to influence government policy, but he or she has got considerable power to sort out the

Above These demonstrators from Help the Aged also wrote to every Member of Parliament protesting about the 1973 Social Security Bill.

odd thing for their constituents." (Interview with editor.)

A woman interviewed by the editor said: "Frankly, I'm very fatalistic about politics. I don't think there's anything you can do to influence policies or decisions. I believe a few people only run Britain and make a pretence of consulting the people, by giving them an election once every four or five years. What can you do? You don't agree with something so you start a campaign or protest, or whatever; but if the powers that be have already made up their minds, then that's it—not a chance. If you've got money, you might have more of a chance. Look how big business and industry behave. They've got influence—they can say we don't like this and government has to pay attention because the country is controlled by them. Money means power and influence and how many of us have that?"

Here a woman in Newcastle-upon-Tyne describes to the editor how she, and other people, formed a tenants' association in their road: "The TA was originally formed because local people were becoming increasingly worried about what was to happen to their houses. The houses are owned and used as revenue for a wealthy church trust and the remaining ninety-nine-year leases on properties in the area have terminated this year and tenants have not been adequately informed of their positions. Contact was made with the city planning department, which had plans for a comprehensive redevelopment of the area, due to the fact that a motorway was to be built alongside this, the only, residential area within the city centre. We also contacted the agent for the landlord, whose apparent aim was to help the tenants in the way that best suited the individual—i.e. 'piecemeal' development. Each house to be modernized according to occupiers' needs. Our association seemed to make great headway during the embryonic stages and found that the planning department, city engineers and landlord were keen to form a good liaison. Repairs were done more rapidly and plans for the area were readily supplied and discussed with the tenants. We were recognized as a small but fairly powerful body. . . . Certainly a great deal has been done through the TA to make the authorities aware of the needs of this area."

Collecting petitions is one way of showing opposition, or support, for an idea or belief. "Mrs Maureen Thomson, a Guildford housewife is leading a campaign to stop Surrey County Council building a new County Hall in the city's Stoke Park. 'The park', she says, 'is a lung, a breathing space in the city, and the erection of a large building would destroy it.' More than 6,000 signatures have been collected by the Save Guildford Committee, to which she belongs, calling for a public inquiry." (*Observer*, 1974.)

Although it is not a suggestion that you take this as an example, here is action that one person can take! What is the point of this sort of action?

"Sir,—I am writing to explain why I felt it necessary to lob a flour bag at Mr Heath [then Prime Minister] before the British Lions' reception recently.

"The issue of racialism in sport was being ignored in the celebration of the Lions victory and the only way to draw attention back to the issue was to do something dramatic. So I chose the flour bag idea, because it would not harm anyone or cause any damage. It is very sad that it is necessary to do this sort of thing in order to get publicity for the non-racial cause, but normal means of protest are increasingly ignored by the media. . . . Yours faithfully, Sally Hain." (*Guardian*, 1974.)

"Ramsay Street, Rochdale, is the sort of place where racial troubles start. The local community relations office says so and the local branch of the National Front thought so when it heard that the white residents were resentful about problems that followed a big influx of Asians.

"Last year a white resident of this conglomeration of old terrace houses and scattered rubbish dumps organized a petition about the horrors of living in the area. She found three members of the National Front on her doorstep.

"She sent them packing but admits now that at the time help from anyone would have seemed attractive if it hadn't been for the safety valve of a meeting with local MP, Cyril Smith, the following day.

"Out of this and several other meetings with councillors and the community relations officer for Rochdale, the Ramsay Street improvement scheme grew up. It is a committee of the residents; whites and new immigrants; and even though its practical achievements are not great so far, it is the kind of organization that, with plenty of local authority help, might make Ramsay Street a happier place for all.

"So far, the improvements are small. Residents say that the dustman call more regularly, the streets are swept, which never happened in the past, and some of the rubbish dumps have been cleared. Immigrant committee members put pressure on their own countrymen to tidy up the back alleys and the outside of their houses." (*Guardian*.)

1. List four ways of protesting about the closure of a cinema in your area, in order of action.

2. Compose a short letter to your local newspaper putting the case *for* more local authority spending on amenities for young people in your area.

3. How could you persuade your local authority to provide help for unemployed school leavers?

Below People signing a petition for the repeal of the Corn Laws. This was a successful campaign to allow cheap grain imports back into Britain in the mid nineteenth century.

Above Is squatting justified when homeless people take over empty houses?

10 Direct action

One important feature of a democracy is that people are given the chance to express their desires, or grumbles, through such things as elections, lobbying or writing to MPs, forming pressure groups and the like. Some feel, however, that these things are just not influential and effective enough—that such methods never achieve results. They believe that it is only through direct action, such as demonstrating, that an impact is made.

Demonstrations (peaceful or violent) have become part of the political scene in this country. Does it mean that people can't get what they want by other means? Or simply that we've become so used to these forms of direct action that they no longer surprise us, but are accepted as an effective means of getting what we want? Or do they really "frighten" or bribe those in authority into doing as they are told?

The Campaign for Nucelar Disarmament (CND) made marching famous as a form of civil disobedience. The Aldermaston marches were common sights over the Easter holidays in the late 1950s and early 1960s. The Campaign's aim was to protest against the manufacture, possession and any possible use of nuclear weapons, and it did so by sitting down, distributing leaflets setting out its aims, holding meetings and by the Aldermaston marches. Annually thousands would march to the Atomic Energy Research Establishment at Aldermaston to protest against the Establishment's work and campaign for nuclear disarmament. Civil disobedience, the non-violent, passive resistance to policies and principles as preached by Gandhi in India, was put into practice in Britain.

Denis Knight, Secretary of the Film and TV Committee for Nuclear Disarmament records, in the only existing diary of the first Aldermaston march, the following description: "Between the regiments of sour and drab fir, planted up to the very edges of the road, there was moving forward a great mass of men, women and children, four or five or six abreast, in a procession that was probably the longest that English roads have seen these centuries on foot, and was certainly the most purposeful. Its purpose was significant not only for England, but for every other country East and West, because it became clearer with every yard walked that this was more than an old-fashioned peace demonstration, more than a spiritual hunger march. It was felt, as we walked almost in silence through these menacing and monotonous woods, that this was above all a civilizing mission, a march away from fear towards normality, towards human standards, towards the real people in the nursery rhyme whose houses are over the hill but not so far away that we will not get there by candlelight, whose hands are set to the plough and the making of things."

Peter Hain organized direct action against a visiting South African rugby team, the Springboks, because he and his followers strongly disagreed with the South African government's policy of apartheid. The direct action group he set up was called Stop the Seventy Tour (the visit was to take place in 1970) and they tried to physically stop the matches taking place by sit downs and by invading the rugby pitches. He describes the growth of his campaign: "Almost overnight, a mass movement sprang up against the rugby tour. . . . There were demonstrations at every one of the twenty-four tour matches; two matches had to be switched from their original venues because the authorities felt that the grounds were indefensible. . . .

"A countrywide campaign developed,

Above Police and marchers clash during an anti-apartheid demonstration against the Springboks' 1969-70 tour.

growing in strength as the tour went on. Intense pressure was exerted on the authorities by the force of the demonstrations in the first month; by the time of the successful disruption of the sixth match at Twickenham, which was stopped for some ten minutes as demonstrators poured on to the pitch, the whole tour was in severe jeopardy. The matches were only able to go on protected by the massive police resources. . . .

"But the tour continued, stumbling through right to the end. After the first month of the three-month itinerary, the grounds were enveloped by a network of security. Then the barbed wire went up around the perimeter of some tour venues—finally the grounds began to assume the appearance of armed camps. Match disruptions, centring around the invasion and sit-down tactics, became more difficult. And, with just over half the tour completed, the campaign organizers decided to extend activities outside the specific area of the matches themselves. Direct action protests were staged at the Springboks' hotels and at the start of their coach journeys. On the morning of the international match at Twickenham on 20th December, an attempt was made to drive the team's coach away. It was only partially successful. But the point was made, and soon afterwards the Springbok manager threatened to take his team home unless security could be increased." (Peter Hain, "Direct Action and the Springbok Tours" in *Direct Action and Democratic Politics*, edited by R Benewick and T Smith.)

"The second day of the renewed Archway road inquiry in north London was abandoned in uproar last night after 90 minutes of astonishing scenes between protesters and Department of Transport witnesses.

"Objectors to the £11m scheme surrounded a group of seven men sitting in the public part of the hall and accused them of being government officials. Mr Ralph Rolph, the harassed inspector, refused a demand that they should be seated elsewhere and adjourned the hearing . . . to shouts of 'spies out'. . . . [Earlier] police were called in to remove a man who jumped on the stage. . . . There were angry exchanges over a refusal by the commissionaires to allow some people into the inquiry. Mr Rolph . . . ordered that everyone should be allowed in.

"The first inquiry was abandoned last autumn after disruption by protesters and the illness of the inspector." (*Times*, 1977.)

Some people feel so frustrated that they have nowhere to live, and that their names are forever on housing waiting lists, that they take matters into their own hands. They take over empty houses and squat there until the council involved either evicts them, or provides them with a home.

There is even a pamphlet written especially for squatters, telling them how to squat, called *The Squatters' Handbook.*

"In the Streets

"It is vital that the people in the street—particularly in the street where you live—should know who you are and what is going on. Publish leaflets . . . as often as you can giving the up-to-date situation—whatever is said in the press, will be distorted and is likely to reflect the landlord's point of view—and distribute them to every house in the neighbourhood, in local pubs, in shopping streets and markets. If you use your petition at the same time you are likelier to get into discussion and be able to put your case and learn what people are thinking. Put up a noticeboard outside your house giving the most recent news; make posters for your windows and to distribute: if you can, do a street comic to serve as a leaflet. Basically you are asking for the support of your neighbours—is there any way in which you can also support them?

"If you have a reasonable amount of local support try holding a street meeting or a street party. . . .

Don't Be Afraid to go Far Out!

"Barricades were used in Islington as an act of insurrection, in which one of the streets, where there was a house threatened with eviction, was blocked to vehicles at both ends and declared a NO GO area. Other people in the street showed their solidarity. . . . A hunger strike (four people fasting for a week each) was held in Islington. It made a focal point for the town hall picket every day. Occupations of the town hall, housing department or housing association office might also be effective."

"Dutch police were last night questioning two Arab hijackers of a BOAC Super VC-10 who commandeered the flight ninety minutes out of Beirut, ordered it to land at Amsterdam and then set fire to whisky which they had poured over the seats.

"The hijackers boarded the flight, which started in Bombay, during a stop-over in Beirut. BOAC chief steward Mr Robin Wright, aged 34, said that the crew had been thoroughly searched at Beirut, but the passengers had apparently been allowed to walk on board the aircraft without much security checking.

"The two hijackers were members of the National Youth for the Liberation of Palestine, an offshoot of Black September. The same group was responsible for the deaths of thirty-two people at Rome and Athens airports last December.

"Last night the plane was isolated at Schipol airport, its interior still smoking.

"Two bombs were later found in the burned-out fuselage of the hijacked VC-10. One was an incendiary device.

"Mr Wright said that the two Arabs, aged

between twenty-five and thirty, rushed into the cockpit armed with very small pistols, and ordered the captain and engineer into the rear economy section of the plane. All first-class passengers were also ordered into the rear seats—a total of about a hundred hostages. Mr Wright said: 'One of the hijackers stayed with the two junior pilots in the cockpit—he had a hand-grenade and a pistol which he aimed at the head of one of the pilots.

"'The other hijacker fired his pistol into a seat in the first class section presumably to show us he meant business. Over the public address system he said: "I am your new captain. I represent Palestine liberation. Put your hands on your heads and sit down and everyone will be OK." The atmosphere was very good—as calm as you can believe,' Mr Wright said.

"The Arabs had said the operation was aimed at Britain and the United States. They warned that more British and American aircraft would be hijacked in the future because the two countries had helped Israel during the Middle East war. . . ." (*Guardian*.)

1. Do you think demonstrations can achieve anything? If so, what?

2. What other action could the Arab hijackers have taken to plead their cause?

3. Do you think their action was justified?

Above The British Super VC-10 at Amsterdam after it was set on fire by Arab hijackers.

11 Should you participate in politics?

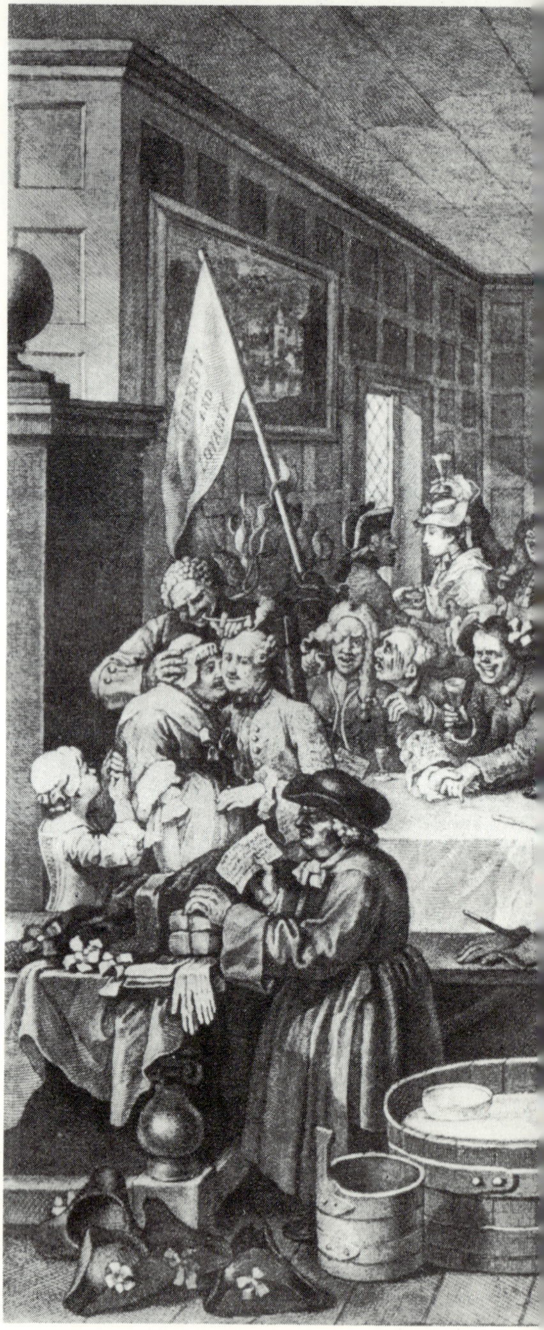

Government in a democracy is said to rest on public opinion. The people are supposed to determine, ultimately, the policies and government of the day. This means that people need to be interested enough in politics to elect MPs and have ideas about what sort of policies they would like to be put into practice. It also means that those who are in positions of authority must be watched and criticized so that they don't overstep their positions of power. Is it, therefore, your duty—if you want this sort of government—to participate in politics? What would happen if you didn't?

A man interviewed by the editor had this to say: "I think I have an obligation to vote at least, because if I derive benefits from a society, such as a health service, old age pensions etc, then I should take an interest in how that society is run. But, I don't feel any need to participate in active politics because that's the job of the people I vote for and their party organization."

"Well, there's a saying that you get the democracy you deserve, and I believe that. If you don't bother to vote you can hardly complain about the lot that's in power when you don't like them. You helped to put them there through your apathy. It's the argument of the silent majority. If you're silent and don't register either a protest or support, then effectively you lend weight to those in authority, and your silence is taken as consent. You don't achieve anything or alter anything by divorcing yourself from politics, unless you want to lead the life of a complete hermit, who has nothing to do with society anyway." (Man interviewed by the editor.)

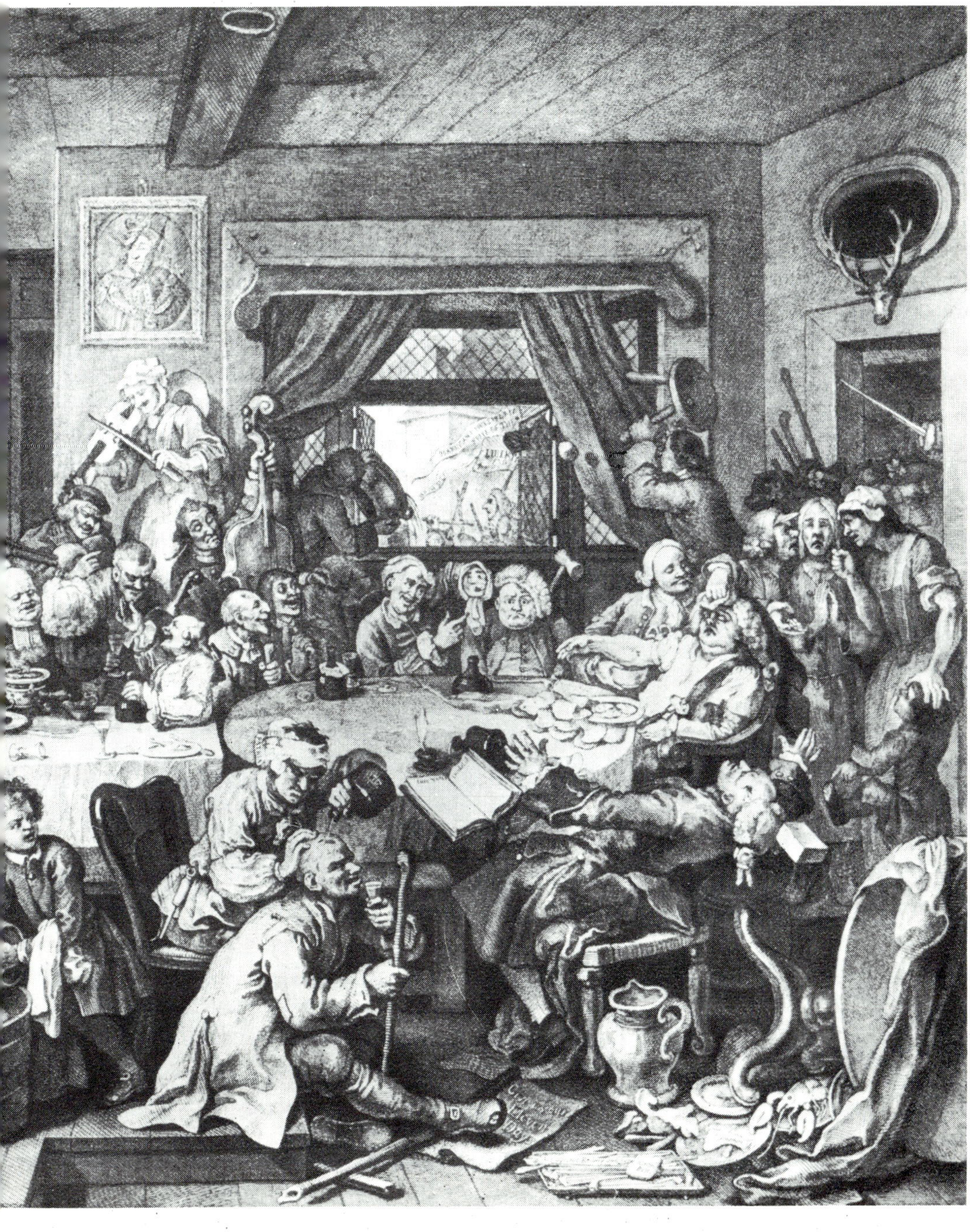

Above Now, people can vote freely in a secret ballot. In the eighteenth century, politicians sometimes bribed or threatened voters. Here is William Hogarth's view of an election day banquet for a politician's supporters.

This selection of interviews from *The Civic Culture* by Almond and Verba gives some more examples of what people think in this country and others. They talk about the ordinary citizen's duty in society.

"**A British housewife:** 'A citizen should take some part in public life and have a say in town planning, education and religion.'

"**An American postmaster:** 'A citizen should play an active part. . . . He might hold a local office. Other civic work such as drives, such as Red Cross. Here we have a volunteer fire company; he could help out with that.'

"**An American housewife:** 'I think a person should vote. If there are any town meetings he should attend them. . . . If everyone does things in his own small way, it would add up to something big. Many people sit back and let others do things for them, then complain.'

"**A German farmer:** 'He should discuss politics, but shouldn't just accept everything but [should] speak up too.'

"**An English businessman:** 'He should help in local organizations—children's clubs, boy scouts. He should help his neighbours and be a good living person.'

"**An English housewife:** 'He ought to know what is going on. Go to the occasional meeting to find out.'

"**A Mexican housewife:** '[He should] be interested in how the government is formed, and be active by studying books and newspapers.'

"**An Italian teacher:** 'Each individual should be interested in an active way and should criticize justly and severely when it is necessary.'

"**An American disabled worker:** 'I think they should do their part. Outside of voting there isn't too much the average fellow can do. . . . You ought to vote and then support any worthwhile thing your community is trying to do.'

"**An Italian veterinarian:** 'What should the individual do? Elect his representatives. That's all.'

"**A German retired worker:** 'Choose a mayor at election time. That's all one need do. The mayor takes care of everything.'

"**A German housepainter:** 'He should vote—that's the most important thing. But he should not be politically active himself.'

"**An English housewife:** 'It's as much as my husband can do to go to work, never mind taking part in local affairs. We appoint councillors and leave everything to them.'

"**A German housewife:** 'We have to work. The people in the council are cleverer after all. They'll do a good job. You just have to vote for the right ones.' "

Stanley Baldwin, Prime Minister at the time, had this to say about participation when he broadcast to schools in March 1934: "Democracy is a most difficult form of government—difficult, because it requires for its perfect functioning the participation of all the people of the country. It cannot function—not function well—unless everyone, men and women alike, feel their responsibility to their State, do their own duty, and try to choose the men who will do theirs. It is not a matter of party: it is common to all of us, because Democracy wants constant guarding."

"No, there's no point in taking part in politics at all. The country will be governed whatever you do. It makes no difference who does it. Whoever it is, they never pay any attention to you—they're there for their own satisfaction, not for any good of humanity. They just like to pretend they're all very liberal and democratic by allowing you to vote occasionally. But, what choice do you have anyway? No, I have nothing to do with it. It makes no odds to me who's in or what they do. I'm sick of the lot of them. Let them get on with it, but leave me out of it." (Housewife, interviewed by the editor.)

John Stuart Mill, a political writer and philosopher of the last century, had this to say about participation: "The passive type of character is favoured by the government of one or a few, and the active self-helping type by that of the many. Irresponsible rulers need the quiescence [acceptance] of the ruled more than they need any activity. . . . Submissiveness . . . is the lesson inculcated by all governments upon those who are wholly without participation in them. . . . But no men are mere instruments or materials in the hands of their rulers who have will or spirit or a spring of internal activity in the rest of their proceedings."

Mill also says that if you do not participate in government then your interests may well be overlooked: ". . . The rights and interests of every or any person are only secure from being disregarded when the person interested is himself able, and habitually disposed, to stand up for them . . . human beings are only secure from evil at the hands of others in proportion as they have the power of being, and are, self-*protecting*." (*Representative Government*.)

"A scheme aimed at encouraging school children to take an interest in local government is being launched by Community Service Volunteers, the young people's community action group.

"The group has devised for use in schools an educational game which it hopes will help to banish the 'boring' image of councils.

"To play the game children have to imagine they are councillors faced with pressing problems to solve. The 'councillors' meet together to discuss alternative courses of action and to decide on which projects should take priority.

"The game is being distributed to schools throughout the country following a trial run in Islington Town Hall. Fourteen children from the Burnt Mill Comprehensive School, Harlow, played the game in the council chamber at the invitation of the borough council and CSV whose headquarters are in Islington.

"Mr Alan Ram, the CSV organizer responsible for organizing the trial run said: 'We had a very successful session. The children entered into the spirit of the thing. I think the game helped them to realize that local government is not a simple matter of providing whatever services residents want. It involves assessing priorities and allocating scarce resources.

" 'The trial run at Islington encourages me to think that the game will be successful in stimulating interest in what at present seems to many children to be a very dreary subject.' " (*Evening Standard*, 1974.)

Would education of this kind make *you* more interested in local government? Would it encourage you to take part in it? Do people need to be educated to participate in politics?

1. What part does the public in this country play in government?

2. Why, according to John Stuart Mill, do governments like "passive" people? Do you think this is true in this country?

3. At what age do you think you should be allowed to vote? Why?

Chapter 2

What are the alternatives?

Developing countries in the process of establishing their political systems often look to Britain as an example of how a democracy should work. The features that are admired are the opportunities for choosing and criticizing government. But not everyone here agrees that Britain has such an enviable political system. Many ordinary people feel that their interests and opinions are overlooked. Others feel that practically the whole system will soon grind to a halt—the process of passing laws being so slow. But what are the alternatives?

In times of economic crisis or war, some people believe that strong leadership is what is really wanted—a benevolent dictator, who would take decisions for us. Is that what most people really want? It certainly would do away with the bother of listening to every side of an argument before reaching a decision, and it would save time. But doesn't strong leadership too often result in the complete suppression of individual rights and beliefs?

If you don't believe that dictatorship is the answer, what other possibilities are there? In order to really change society some say that revolution—the violent overthrow of a government—is the only answer. Such people think that the peaceful methods of influencing government never have any effect. But if you don't believe in violence and prefer to look to a time when all people can live peacefully together, what do you do? Is it, for instance, possible for different nations to unite and perhaps form some kind of international or world government? The United Nations Organization and the European Economic Community are both international bodies, and examples of how different nations can work together; but could governmental co-operation ever exist on a world scale?

Of course you could escape from government altogether. You could create an ideal, self-supporting community of your own, and run it the way *you* want. Or, as anarchists believe, you could get rid of all forms of government, all rules, laws and rulers. Why not rely on the individual's good sense and let people get on with running their own lives? Could this really work? Can we now do without any form of government? Or are we, willingly or not, inescapably bound to the need for government in our complex society?

Right The United Nations Building in New York. Is this a first step towards world government?

1 What is wrong with our system of government?

Do you like the way our political system works, or not? There are many complaints levelled at it—by the ordinary man or woman in the street and by politicians themselves. The voter often feels left out, that he has little say in decision making. Politicians sometimes feel the party system is too narrow, or that government is over-centralized in London. These are a few of the complaints levelled at it. What are the good things about it?

"One of the principal reasons for the present disillusionment with politics and politicians in this country is the over-centralized government structure, when essentially local problems have to be continually referred to Whitehall. . . . Local government has insufficient power, money and influence; the rise of bureaucratic management results in Whitehall being incapable of handling all its business; and Parliament is unable to control government effectively and is also hamstrung by lack of time. The overall result is ineffective, slow and inefficient government." (*Power to the People*, Liberal Party Report.)

Many people in Scotland and Wales, and indeed in the regions of England, complain that government is too concentrated in London. They would like to see power devolved to local areas, where people who know and understand the problems specific to such areas can deal with them, and where there is more chance for participation by the people themselves. Some, such as the Nationalists in Scotland and Wales, want a complete break from the British Government so that they can exist as independent states. Others just want more power and responsibility in the hands of regional governments. The Labour Government in 1976 responded by suggesting certain devolution measures:

"The time is now right for reforms making our system of government more democratic, more accountable and more open to the people. Labour recognizes that this is especially true of Scotland and Wales. In these countries a conscious sense of their own national identities within the United Kingdom adds distinct flavour and urgency to the demand for ordinary Scottish and Welsh people to be given a fuller say in the running of their public affairs. . . . The Labour Party is pledged to introduce legislation in 1976, to reach the statute book in 1977, which will provide for radically new power structures rooted in Scotland and Wales. . . .

"We propose massive handovers of power to new directly-elected Scottish and Welsh Assemblies seated at Edinburgh and Cardiff. The Assemblies will wield control over key decisions crucial to the everyday life and prospects of every Scots and Welsh family." (*Labour's Programme for Britain*, 1976.)

A major criticism of our system of government is concerned with the electoral system. At present a single Member of Parliament is elected for each constituency by the first-past-the-post method. In other words, the candidate with the most votes in a constituency wins and is elected. This apparently simple method has been defended because, by and large, it has led to stable government based on a majority in Parliament of one party, rather than a coalition of parties. Also it is the system that we have used for a very long time, and therefore the British people know it, understand and accept it. Of prime importance, too, is the very close relationship each MP can have with his constituents. Members of Parliament directly represent all

Right Should we change our electoral system? Or should we go on electing the candidate with the most votes for each constituency?

Left top Is government over-centralized in London?

Below Should there be national assemblies in Scotland and Wales, and more decisions taken in county halls like this one in Lewes?

their constituents, even those who did not vote for them, and thus act as an important link between the individual and central government.

However, there are very strong arguments against the present system. The Hansard Society for Parliamentary Government published a report (the *Blake Report*) which recommended that our electoral system should be reformed. Their reasons for this recommendation rested on some very clear faults inherent in the system.

The *Blake Report* emphasized that in a democracy the electoral system must protect the majority of electors, or at least of voters, from flagrant minority rule. It instances various occasions where there has obviously been unfair representation.

"In February 1974 Liberals polled 19.3 per cent of the vote, or more than half the vote of either of the two larger parties, but gained a mere 14 seats as against 297 for the Conservatives and 301 for Labour."

"In 3 out of the last 13 elections (1929, 1951, February 1974) the party which returned the largest number of MPs had a smaller share of the vote than the runner up party in the House."

"In October 1974, the Labour party obtained an overall majority in terms of seats, yet its percentage share of the total vote (39.2 per cent) was, apart from February 1974, the lowest percentage it recorded since 1935."

"I don't think government is flexible enough, it's too rigid and slow. Look, a problem emerges, discrimination against women in jobs for instance—which has been in existence since the year dot. How long has it taken them to do something about it? While they hummed and hahed about it, many women over the decades, indeed the centuries, have suffered from this particular form of discrimination. The point is, government just takes ages and ages before it does anything. It cannot act speedily, even when the situation obviously demands quick action. It ignores the problem for a long time, hoping it will go away. Then, when pressure is put on it, it sets up a committee of inquiry which sits deliberating for months, if not years. Finally it might get round to preparing a bill on the matter which has to wait its turn, along with all the other legislation that's to be considered. By the time it's introduced it's in a very watered down form, for fear of too much opposition. And, it's probably an inadequate piece of legislation into the bargain. What we need is flexible, efficient, but alert government." (Woman interviewed by editor.)

"The trouble with government, dear, is that it's not strong enough. Government's there to govern. But it doesn't do that. It's like a straw in the wind, blown about by the biggest force. You know who it is who runs this country? The unions. They hold the government to ransom." (Man interviewed by editor.)

"Governments are by and for the rich, the privileged. It's not for, or by the people—as it should be in a democracy. The people come last in the Government's list of priorities. Government is more concerned with other countries, with defence, with maintaining its status abroad. It ought to see to its own house first." (Woman interviewed by editor.)

The *Guardian* discusses another criticism: "There is . . . a vast amount of information that government refuses to reveal for a multiplicity of reasons ranging from potential embarrassment to claims that it would damage commercial confidence. If you want to know, for example, the names of garages struck off the official register of approved testing stations for 'fraud, incompetence or dishonesty', it's no good asking the Department of the Environment. Nor will they tell you which cars have had to be recalled with potentially lethal safety defects or which factories have been warned for dangerous levels of pollution, though all this information is available.

"The Public Expenditure Committee has tried hard to unravel Concorde's financial mess but even this Select Committee of the Commons has found it hard to penetrate the veils of secrecy surrounding the project. Its last report was dotted with asterisks because the Government insisted that the precise figures if published would be damaging to Concorde's commercial prospects. Ordinary MPs are even less able to get at the facts. Parliamentary questions are so easily evaded and so hedged by meaningless rigmarole that an agile minister has little to fear. The Public Interest Research Centre in a report [in 1973] noted, moreover, there were nearly a hundred subjects on which questions cannot even be asked under the Speaker's rules because successive governments have refused to respond to them. The taboo subjects range from telephone tapping to rents for government offices, from details of export licences to the reasons for refusal to refer mergers to the Monopolies Commission."

The concept of the public's right to know is not one that comes easily to either governments or their civil servants. Andrew Shonfield [the economist] put his finger squarely on part of the problem: "The element of arrogance," he wrote, "should not be left out of the compound. Persons who carry high responsibility in Britain tend to assume that they cannot be expected to explain their actions fully to ordinary people, who would be unable to understand even if they wished to. This is the residue of old-fashioned aristocratic principle which remains firmly embedded in British democracy." (*Encounter*.)

Not everyone criticizes our system, however: "The Prince of Wales today defended the system of democratic government in an address to the New South Wales Legislative Council on the occasion of its 150th anniversary. He said that the special brand of parliamentary democracy enjoyed in Australia and Britain had an extraordinary capacity for improvisation, evolution and change.

"The Prince read a message of congratulation from the Queen to the Parliament, which was Australia's first, and then said: 'Despite cries that our system is on the point of collapse, it is rare to hear of anyone who has been able to suggest a sensible or realistic alternative suitable to our type of heritage.

" 'The truth is, of course, that the system is on the whole basically sound. The very fact that the monarchy is involved in the lives of a substantial number of different peoples all over the globe means that it must in effect try to be all things to all men all of the time.

" 'To achieve this kind of adaptation takes time, tact, patience, sensitivity and good taste on all sides, and a measure of mutual understanding.' Throughout his address, the Prince of Wales illustrated his arguments with historical references to King John and the Magna Carta, Cromwell and King Charles 1." (*Times*, 1974.)

"The best thing that can be said about our system of government is that it works. Can you honestly think of any other country in the world where you'd like to live—from a political point of view? I know there are things wrong with this country, but just think what we've got; we've got a national health service, a social security system if

Right David Steel, leader of the Liberal Party, has a special interest in proportional representation.

we're ill, old or out of work, we've got the right to say and do more or less as we like, we can choose who will form a government, fairly regularly, we can criticize them, depose them, form groups to influence them and laugh at them. Above all we can be individuals. Not many people can say all of these things about their country. It's got its faults, but I wouldn't swap it for anywhere else, mate." (Man interviewed by the editor.)

1. Why do you think people become politicians?

2. How could government be improved if it was decentralized, with people in Scotland, Wales and Northern Ireland, and even in large counties, having more say in the running of their areas?

3. Why do you think the law-making process is so slow? Does it have to be?

4. Do you think government should be more open, and that we should be told more about what goes on?

5. What are the good things about our system of government?

6. Suppose you were advising the leader of a new country about important things to include in its political system. What would you say?

2 Would you prefer a dictator?

Dictatorship means that one man or woman at the head of a state rules a country. He takes the decisions concerning domestic and foreign policies, supposedly in people's best interests. But how does one manage to rule over so many, and keep the many from questioning, criticizing or replacing him? Or is it the case that some people prefer someone to lead them, to take decisions for them? Is dictatorship merely strong leadership, or does it go beyond that into the realms of tyranny and totalitarianism?

A dictator necessarily has immense power and he can use this power either for his people's own good, in a benevolent fashion, or he can use it to suppress all opposition. The latter often can mean that criticism, choice, individual freedom are not tolerated. Indeed they can be strictly curtailed. President Amin of Uganda took over power after a *coup d'état* in January 1970, when the then President, Obote, was out of the country. It is said by some that Amin immediately took brutal steps to eliminate Obote supporters, and has subsequently crushed all opposition in a similar way. David Martin, in the *Observer* of 15th August, 1976 said this:

"The slaughter in Uganda began immediately [after the *coup d'etat*]. One of the first to die was Brigadier Suleiman Hussein, the army chief of staff who had led attempts to prevent the *coup d'etat*. He was beaten and hideously mutilated by . . . soldiers in Upper Luzira maximum security prison. A servant at the 'command post', as Amin's house is known, said later that Hussein's severed head was brought to Amin who put it on a table and spoke to it, then kept it in his fridge overnight. Of the twenty-three officers with the rank of lieutenant-colonel and above at the time, fourteen are known to have been murdered and two escaped into exile. Several were among a group of thirty-two officers who were crammed into a tiny cell at Makindye Prison in Kampala and blown up with dynamite on 5th March, 1971."

David Martin goes on to describe how evidence presented to the United Nations by the International Commission of Jurists maintains that "It is impossible to describe the reign of terror which prevails in Uganda. Every village, clan and family has lost relatives and friends. The faces and names of the killers are known; but no one acts. It is as if Uganda is paralysed by fear."

President Tito of Yugoslavia is regarded by many in a different light. He, too, has a strong character, but it is one that many Yugoslavs are grateful for: "By 1969 Yugoslavia had been modernized and developed to the extent that her rate of growth no longer qualified her for the title of underdeveloped country. In spite of backward areas, poverty, unemployment and inequalities, the Yugoslav people were in general well-pleased with the changes brought by Tito's revolution. Modern blocks of flats, washing machines, televisions, new roads, motor cars, traffic jams, an unfavourable balance of payments, rising prices all proclaimed Yugoslavia at one with many contemporary developments in modern industrial society. In spite of some limitation on political activity and on publication of political views, Yugoslavs were in no doubt whatever that their situation was far easier, freer and more prosperous than that of the inhabitants of other communist states. . . .

"[Tito] has never accepted the ideas of multi-party government, believing that these would result in a splintering of political life into regional and factional interests that could destroy . . . the state. This might lead to western-type democracy, or to Russian

Left President Idi Amin of Uganda—a modern dictator who rules by terror.

intervention to impose Soviet-type communism. He would regard either as a disaster. These considerations, especially the fear of Russia, explain why Tito has received such universal support in Yugoslavia. He has been a guarantee of stability, of fighting leadership and political sense; someone who has won, and kept, people's trust, someone to whom difficult problems of political life can be referred, with the confident knowledge that he would do his best to find a just and equitable solution." (Phyllis Auty, *Tito*.)

Mao Tse-tung was another remarkable man, whose achievements were monumental, whether you sympathized with his philosophy or not.

"From a century on which figures like Lenin, Hitler and Stalin have left gigantic imprints—or gigantic wounds—Mao Tse-tung emerges as the last colossus. He shook not only China but the entire postwar world into a strange shape that would have seemed preposterous only thirty years ago. Like the other tyrants, too, he attempted the daunting task of changing human nature. It is still too early to say that he achieved this, but within a quarter of a century he transformed the corrupt, backward, plundered wreck of an empire into a nuclear power and a sovereign state in which a fifth of the population of the planet were united under centralized Communist rule. . . .

"The achievements of the Chinese since Mao came to power in 1949 are astonishing by any standard. They have fed, clothed, housed and educated themselves with minimum help from outside. They have devised a system which provides guarantees for a fifth of the world's population against starvation, homelessness and unemployment. . . . They have virtually eradicated poverty, ignorance and disease. All this has been done, as far as one can tell, with little bloodshed, at least since the immediate aftermath of the civil war. And yet . . . a price has been paid. Any questioning of the system, any attempt at the free play of intelligence or imagination, has been suppressed. Individualism, privacy, have been checked. Human potential has been deliberately stifled. A rigid moral puritanism has been imposed. Mao's China came to resemble a giant schoolroom, from which the mysteries of adult life, the terrors of choice, were firmly excluded." (*Observer*, 1976.)

1. General de Gaulle once said that men need to be ordered. He said that because man was a political animal he had to have organization, orders and leaders. Do you think this is so, or do you think people are capable of running their own lives?

2. Do all dictators have characteristics in common?

3. Do you think it is right to suppress individualism in order to attain a better life for the majority of people?

4. Would Britain benefit from a dictator?

Right Chairman Mao, who led China out of poverty—at a price.

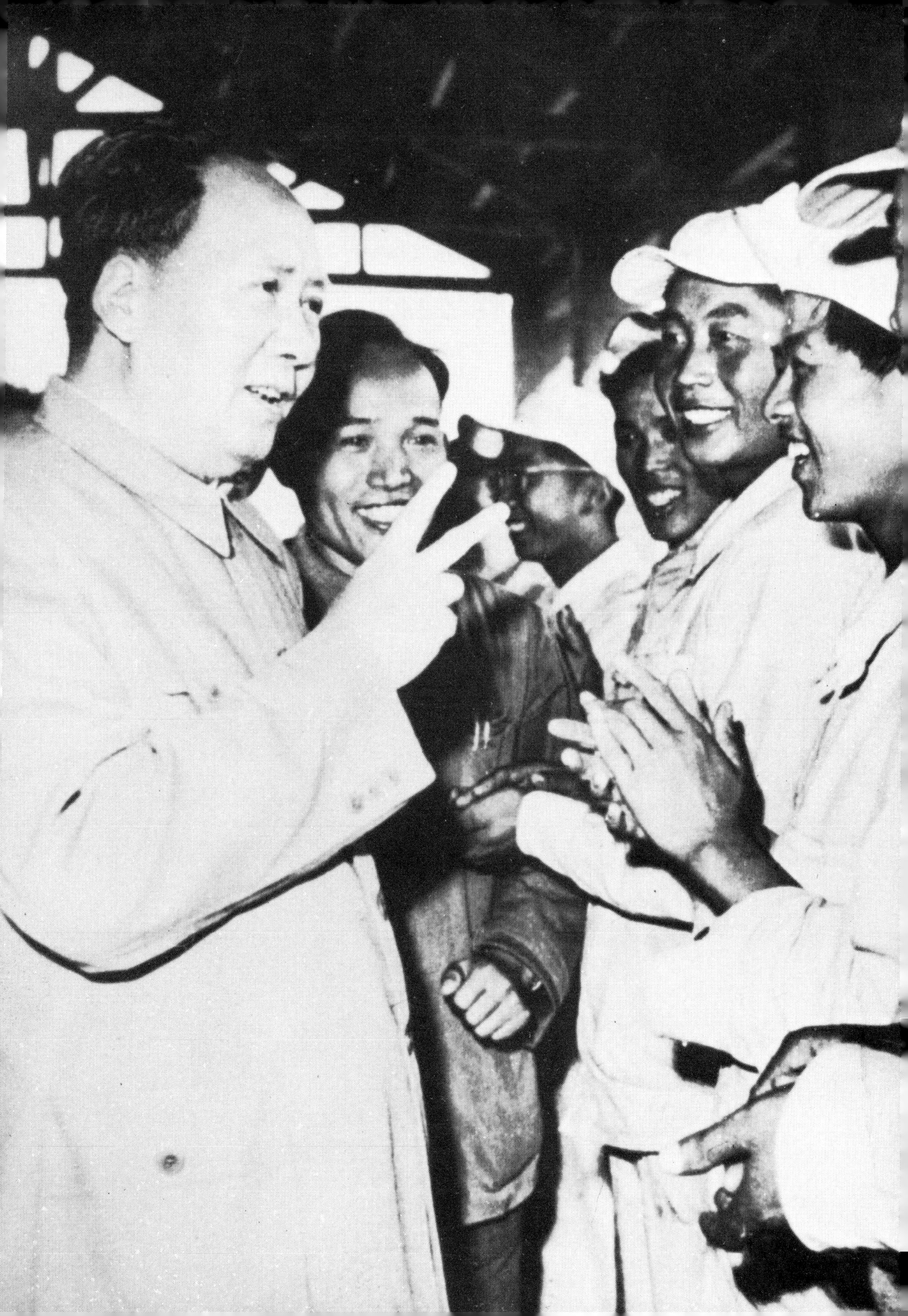

3 Is international government possible?

Is international, and even world, government possible? Many believe that the future of the human race depends very much on the formation of some kind of world government, in which national differences are second ary to the well-being of all humanity. Political union of this kind is seen as the only lasting way to prevent wars and to ensure the progress of mankind. Others, however, see this as being totally unrealistic, and point to the limitations of such organizations as the Common Market. They believe that people will always put national interests above all else.

"I myself have always believed that peace will not be permanently assured until there has been created a world instrument endowed with the necessary authority to maintain the rule of law. That would be our objective." (Selwyn Lloyd, Secretary of State for Foreign Affairs, 1955-60.)

"We must aim at nothing less than the creation of a world authority backed by a world police force, and we must all be prepared to surrender whatever element of national sovereignty this may involve." (Duncan Sandys, Secretary of State for Commonwealth Relations, 1960-64.)

"The only alternative to the hydrogen bomb is some form of world organization resembling and having many powers of a world government." (*New York Times*, 7th July, 1961.)

(All quoted in *The Unification of the World* by Paul de Hevesy.)

"It is only now that we begin to realize the real scale and profundity of the changes in the conditions of human life that are in progress. . . . The scale of distances has

Above The European Economic Community—the Common Market—is an example of economic co-operation. But is political union possible—or desirable?

Above The nine EEC countries — West Germany, France, Italy, Belgium, Luxembourg, Netherlands, Britain, Ireland and Denmark — decide common policy in this magnificent building in Brussels.

been so altered, the physical power available has become so vast, that the separate sovereignty of existing states has become impossible." (H G Wells, *A Short History of the World*.)

"The chief argument in favour of world government is that, if suitably constituted, it can prevent war. . . .

"If world government is to be successfully established there will have to be much more tolerance than there is at present between different kinds of national government. . . . Each nation may continue to *think*, as each nation does at present, that it is superior to all other nations in every essential respect, but, when nations meet for purposes of negotiation, the negotiators will have to restrain public expression of their feelings of superiority within the limits of courtesy." (Bertrand Russell, *Has Man a Future?*)

Hitler deeply believed, however, in almost the complete opposite of internationalism, of different countries carrying on friendly relations, and even wrote: "Our people must be delivered from the hopeless confusion of international convictions and educated consciously and systematically to fanatical nationalism . . . we [must] deliver the people from the atmosphere of pitiable belief in possibilities which lie outside the bounds of one's own strength—such as belief in reconciliation, understanding, world peace . . . and international solidarity—we destroy these ideas. There is only one right in the world and that right is man's own strength." (Quoted in *Hitler: a Study in Tyranny* by Alan Bullock.)

During the First World War there were great feelings of patriotism and romanticism about the country. The idea of fighting for your country became the standard by which heroism and bravery were judged. It was good to fight and even die for England. The poet Rupert Brooke captured this popular feeling in his poem *The Soldier:*

"If I should die, think only this of me:
That there's some corner of a foreign field
That is for ever England."

The European Economic Community, the Common Market, is a working example of how national differences can be overcome, as different countries unite for common goals. Or is it?

The winter fuel crisis in 1973-74 when the Middle East countries withheld oil supplies, produced national differences, not a united front, about the world's energy problems.

"The European Community is in deep crisis here tonight with France entirely isolated from all her partners, including Britain, and with the West German Finance Minister, Herr Schmidt, daring to pronounce the unpronouncable and suggesting that the break-up of the Community can no longer be counted out.

"Britain desperately hopes the setback will not turn out to be quite so profound. After France systematically rejected all suggestions for compromise, the EEC countries at the Washington Energy Conference had to abandon their daylong search for a common position in answer to United States proposals for a co-operative effort in dealing with the energy crisis.

"All the EEC countries, with the exception of France, agree that the major oil consuming countries must work together and prepare for a dialogue with the oil producers. British forces feel that logic seems to have departed from the French on this occasion." (*Guardian*, 13th February, 1974.)

"Sir,—Oil supplies are being withheld from Holland by a number of Arab states.

"The EEC countries ought to formulate immediately a policy to ensure that a member state does not suffer alone when singled out for pressure in this way.

"I look for a swift and firm lead from Britain on this issue." (Letter to the *Guardian*, from David Goodall, Hebrew University, Jerusalem.)

Others, such as Enoch Powell, criticize the British membership of the EEC because they believe it takes power away from both Westminster and the British people.

"This is the first and last election at which the British people will be given the opportunity to decide whether their country is to remain a democratic nation, governed by the will of its own electorate expressed in its own Parliament, or whether it will become one province in a new European super State under institutions which know nothing of the political rights and liberties that we have so long taken for granted.

"Eighteen months ago at the Paris summit conference, this country was committed by the Prime Minister to 'economic and monetary union by 1980' with the rest of the European Economic Community.

"That means that, so far as this Conservative Government is concerned, the lifetime of the next Parliament will see the governance of Britain throughout the whole range of monetary and economic affairs, transferred from Whitehall and Westminster to European authorities, whose decisions will take uniform effect throughout the territory of the present nine states.

"In fulfilling this commitment to 'economic and monetary union by 1980', not the slightest regard will be had to the House of Commons or to the wishes of the electorate." (Enoch Powell in the *Observer*, 1974.)

The United Nations is another example of

Right A Commonwealth Prime Ministers' meeting in London. The Commonwealth is another example of international co-operation.

how different nations can work together to achieve common aims. Its range of activities stretches from peace-keeping roles to medical, economic, cultural and social help in underdeveloped countries. Its purposes are:

"To take effective collective measures for maintaining international peace.

"To develop friendly relations among nations, based on respect for the principle of equal rights and self-determination.

"To achieve co-operation in solving international problems of an economic, social, cultural or humanitarian character, and in promoting respect for human rights and fundamental freedoms without distinction as to race, sex, language or religion.

"To be a centre for harmonizing the actions of nations in attaining these common ends." (Harvey and Bather, *The British Constitution*.)

1. "The war drum throbb'd no longer,
and battle-flags were furled,
In the Parliament of man
the Federation of the world."
The poet Tennyson said this. Do you think that (a) world government would stop wars? (b) that world government is possible?

2. Would you like Britain to be a member of a world government, or would you prefer the country to remain a nation on its own?

3. Do you feel as if you are primarily British, European or simply part of the human race?

4 What can revolutions achieve?

Revolution is the violent overthrow of a regime, and it is favoured by those who believe that such violent action is the only way in which society will ever change. The gradual change of a society by laws, over a long period of time, is scorned: revolutionaries want change now.

Mao Tse-tung, Chairman of China from 1949-1976, said this about revolutions: "A revolution is not a dinner party, or writing an essay, or painting a picture, or doing embroidery; it cannot be so refined, so leisurely and gentle, so temperate, kind, courteous, restrained and magnanimous. A revolution is an insurrection, an act of violence by which one class overthrows another. A rural revolution is a revolution by which the peasantry overthrows the power of the feudal landlord class." (from "Report on an Investigation of the Peasant Movement in Hunan" March 1972 in *Selected Works of Mao Tse-tung*.)

But what happens after revolutions? Do they achieve a better way of life? Or do they replace one undesirable way of living with another? Why are they necessary anyway?

Elizabeth Sutherland Martinez visited Cuba after the revolution, interviewed people, and wrote about their views, and her own, in a book called *The Youngest Revolution*: "Before the revolution, Cuba was a colony: poor and underdeveloped. . . . It was a society of Haves bossing Have-Nots . . . a society of white supremacists and male supremacists. The majority of people scraped out an existence while a city-based minority held hands with Uncle Sam [the USA] to their mutual benefit. That minority, the ruling class, created a subclass of rulers who sat in offices and thought of 'the people' as document numbers (and nuisances). . . . Cuba is no longer a society of Haves oppressing Have-Nots. The country is run in the interests of 'the people', meaning the agricultural and industrial workers who form the vast majority of its population. By 1967, seventy per cent of its agricultural production, all of its heavy industry, foreign trade, education, and culture were state-owned. . . .

"Things like rent, education, medical and dental care, places for women to leave their children while they work—those are just not problems that you normally think about. Those things are all free, except for the medicines themselves in some cases. Some people still pay ten per cent rent, but many have already been given title to their homes. Lots of little things have become free too, like sports events. And calls from public telephones—that just happened last week.

"There are still certain kinds of injustices. Too many bureaucrats have a comfortable niche and they protect it. When something wrong happens, they don't challenge anybody—they don't speak up. They just go along with it, protecting their jobs and homes. There is an opportunism which bothers me a lot. And Havana is the land of gossip, what we call *tiqui-tiqui*. It is easy to ruin a person here—his name is mentioned, somebody lifts an eyebrow, and soon fifty eyebrows are being lifted."

The playwright George Bernard Shaw did not believe in changing societies by revolutions. Apart from the horror and violence they inevitably breed, he saw them as essentially impractical: "Every bumptious idiot thinks himself a born ruler of men; every snob thinks that the common people must be kept in their present place or shot down if society is to be preserved; every proletarian [worker] who resents his position wants to strike at something or somebody . . . but when they have all done their worst the dead they have slain must be buried, the houses

Right Even after the revolution, life is not one baseball game for the Cubans. The striker is their Prime Minister, Fidel Castro.

they have burned rebuilt, and the hundred other messes they have left cleared by women and men with sense enough to take counsel together without coming to blows, and business ability enough to organize the work of the community. These sensible ones may not always have been sensible: some of them may have done their full share of mischief before the necessary sanity was branded into them by bitter experience or horrified contemplation of the results of anarchy; but between the naturally sensible people and the chastened ones there will finally be some sort of Parliament to conduct the nation's business, unless indeed civilization has been so completely wrecked in the preliminary quarrels that there is no business to transact." (*Intelligent Woman's Guide*.)

John Gerassi, editor of a book about revolutions called *Towards Revolution*, has a different view: "When reforms are not enough to satisfy the discontent, the ruling class inevitably resorts to reaction, inevitable precisely because the reforms demanded require the ruling class to commit class suicide. It is as if we demanded that all cars produced be indestructible, unpolluting and cheap (all technologically feasible). General Motors, Ford, the oil and insurance companies would obviously object. They're in business to make profits, which they use to maintain their life style. If people's demands grew louder, they might try a few reforms; more padding, better seat belts, a special carburettor which cuts down pollution and a policy of recalling cars to fix

major defects at their expense (all of which they've done or are doing). But suppose we still weren't satisfied—you and me and the other fodder—and our discontent grew to the point that we were willing to seize General Motors, burn down the insurance companies. . . . Then what? Well, Ford and General Motors bosses are certainly not going to give up their yachts and planes and villas in eight countries, nor the control they exercise through their wealth over every institution in the land. They'll tell their representatives (the government) to put an end to the dissent and the government will then try to jail or kill us. Our only alternative is revolution."

A Russian called Yury Krotkov defected to the West because he could not stand the kind of society that the revolution produced. He describes the kind of procedure that a Russian citizen had to go through simply to get permission to travel abroad: "Room 211 was something like a reading room in a small public library—twenty or thirty little tables, each with a writing set. Five or six people were sitting there. It was absolutely quiet. In the corner, at a large desk, sat an ascetic-looking, grey-haired woman. I told her I came from Startsev.

"'Where are you travelling?' she asked dryly.

"'To Belgium and to Luxembourg.'

"She wrote down my surname and the countries I had named; then she gave me the instructions and the obligations.

"'Read them and fill this out!'

"I sat down at the table. I glanced at the instructions (stamped 'Top Secret') and became frightened yet again. They listed the rules for the behaviour of 'Soviet patriots' abroad in exhausting detail, cited the recruitment methods of foreign intelligence services, reminded us, for example, that we should not visit restaurants, shops and cinemas alone, that we should refuse to be in the same train compartment as a woman, that during conversations in hotel rooms we should turn on the tap to drown the sound of our voices. There was also mention of guarding documents, and avoiding family quarrels. At the end came an abundance of moral and Party exhortations. Ugh! All this intended for brainless idiots, for slaves, for degenerates! Nothing was left to a man's conscience, to his discretion, to his talent. This was a self-instruction book for apes, for semi-mechanical robots.

"Having 'acquainted' myself with the instructions in this way, I signed the obligation (also stamped 'Top Secret') that I would follow the recommendations in every way. Once more I was warned that if I violated the instructions, a terrible punishment would await me. . . .

"Looking back at the massive grey building, I thought in horror, but what if communism should triumph throughout the world. . . . What would happen then? The world would be ruled by people who live for a system and to whom all other systems seem not only unacceptable, but criminal. This whole police system of oppression and disparagement of the human personality would triumph, and ultimately it would strangle the very nature of man." (Yuri Krotkov, *Angry Exile*.)

But life before the revolution, in Russia, was also hard.

"The twentieth century had come painfully to Russia. . . . [She] remained, despite her economic advances, predominantly a nation of peasants. Only forty years before the turn of the century they had been serfs living in medieval bondage, and many of the attributes of serfdom still clung to them. Even when they moved to the towns to join the new working class, they either had to give up all their land rights, or they were

Left Starving peasants in pre-revolutionary Russia marching to St Petersburg.

compelled to return each year to their villages for the harvest. So they became neither real peasants nor real proletarians, just unskilled casual labourers. Their poverty was chronic; wages were pitifully low, working hours were long; health and safety regulations were practically non-existent; there were no trade unions, no right to strike. In the countryside, the peasants were increasingly irked by the restrictions which governed their lives and coveted the ownership of land. In country and town alike there was mounting discontent, to which the autocracy knew only one answer: repression.

"Under the autocracy political parties were not permitted—though that did not prevent them from existing. But there was no parliament or national assembly which they could try to control by general elections, or, as an opposition, where they could voice the people's demands. . . ." (John Terraine, *The Mighty Continent*.)

Klaus Mehnert has visited China since the Communists gained power, and gives examples of how attitudes have changed in his book *China Today*: ". . . A woman doctor . . . was working at a clinic in Peking. There, all her patients were city people. She looked down her nose at the peasants. They were dirty, she said. She . . . was criticized by the masses and came to us. [A 'school' designed to help people go back to a simple life, and live 'closer to the masses'.] Life here was not easy for her, but she tried her best. When one of the peasant women was sick she moved in with her in order to give her better care. Here she did some of the dirtiest jobs herself, and so she got rid of her prejudices.

". . . Out of love for Chairman Mao and the well-being of the Chinese people and our socialist fatherland, we must be ready to take on the heaviest burdens and do the most repellent jobs. What is the most repellent thing one can do? Cleaning the latrines. So, each of us has to do this job, not only here but also back home in the city. One of the men here was the deputy chairman of East Peking. There, of course, every child knew him. So it was a particular ordeal for him to go back to his own section of the city, where he had been one of the top leaders, and come in all dusty and sweaty after a long march, to empty the latrines there. He was afraid he would lose face entirely. But he overcame his revulsion and did like the others; he emptied the latrines and shoved the stinking buckets onto his cart to bring them twenty km back here, so that the

Above Teachers and students helping farm workers with the harvest on a Chinese commune.

contents could be spread on the school's fields. He had come to understand, you see, that emptying the latrines is not a dirty job, but honourable work. . . .

"That's the main thing about our school; here we have no officialdom, no rank, we are all students, workers in the heat of the summer as the cold of winter."

1. Revolutions inevitably imply violence. Can you think of a situation in which such violence is justifiable, or not? What, if anything, would make you revolt?

2. Do you think that people— as in the example from *China Today*— ought to be made to do things for the general good of the community?

3. Yuri Krotkov defected from Russia to the West because he didn't like the society that eventually followed the revolution. What would you have done in his circumstances?

5 Life without a government

Suppose you don't really like the idea of any form of government—what can you do then? Well, you could form a self-sufficient community of your own, run in the way you choose. Or you could go right away from civilization, to some forgotten island and live without the rules and regulations of organized society. Or, as the anarchists believe, you could fight for the abolition of all forms of government. They don't believe in laws or leaders; instead they put their faith in the ability and reason of the individual to run his own life the way he wants. Are any of these possible?

Robert Owen, a pioneer of the Co-operative and Socialist movements, wrote a book in 1813 called *A New View of Society*. In it, he describes how he believes a community could be organized, and gives as an example a cotton-manufacturing community at New Lanark, Scotland. Owen believed that men's characters are formed by the kind of environment in which they are brought up and live, and also the way they are treated. In this example, the community has just got a new manager, who, by improving the personal relationships, and circumstances, in the community, improves the people too.

"The manager . . . spent some time in finding out the full extent of the evil against which he had to contend, and in tracing the true causes which had produced . . . [the bad] effects. He found that all was distrust, disorder, and disunion; and he wished to introduce confidence, regularity, and harmony. He therefore began to bring forward his various expedients to withdraw the unfavourable circumstances by which they had hitherto been surrounded, and to replace them by others calculated to produce a more happy result. He soon discovered that theft was extended through almost all the community, and the receipt of stolen goods through all the country around. To remedy this evil, not one legal punishment was inflicted, not one individual imprisoned, even for an hour; but checks and other regulations of prevention were introduced; a short plain explanation of the immediate benefits they would derive from a different conduct was inculcated by those instructed for the purpose, who had the best powers of reasoning among themselves. They were at the same time instructed how to direct their industry in legal and useful occupations, by which, without danger or disgrace, they could really earn more than they had previously obtained by dishonest practices. . . .

"Drunkenness was attacked in the same manner; it was discountenanced on every occasion by those who had charge of any department: its destructive and pernicious effects were frequently stated . . . when the individual was soberly suffering from the effects of his previous excess; pot and public houses were gradually removed from the immediate vicinity of their dwellings; the health and comfort of temperance were made familiar to them; by degrees drunkenness disappeared. . . .

"Falsehood and deception met with a similar fate: they were held in disgrace: their practical evils were shortly explained; and every countenance was given to truth and open conduct. . . .

"Dissensions and quarrels . . . when they could not be readily adjusted between the parties themselves, they were stated to the manager; and as in such cases both disputants were usually more or less in the wrong, that wrong was in as few words as possible explained, forgiveness and friendship recommended, and one simple and easily remembered precept inculcated, as the most valuable rule for their whole conduct . . . 'That in future they should endeavour to use the same active exertions to make each other happy and comfortable,

Right top The school at New Lanark.
Below A paradise?

as they had . . . done to make each other miserable. . . .' During the period that these changes were going forward, attention was given to the domestic arrangements of the community. Their houses were rendered more comfortable, their streets were improved, the best provisions were purchased and sold to them at low rates. . . . Fuel and clothes were obtained for them in the same manner; and no advantage was attempted to be taken of them, or means used to deceive them.

"In consequence, their . . . full confidence was obtained, and they became satisfied no evil was intended them; they were convinced that a real desire existed to increase their happiness. . . . They were taught to be rational, and they acted rationally."

Some people like to think of escaping from our civilized society altogether; rather than creating ideals for different kinds of societies, they go off to far away places, in search of a more primitive, yet more peaceful, existence.

"Back to nature? Farewell to civilization? It is one thing to dream of it, and another to do it. I have actually done it.

"With my young wife, Liv, I ran away from bureaucracy, technology, and the grip of twentieth-century civilization. She was twenty, and I was twenty-two. Today this experience would be a hippy's dream, a trip deep into an utterly different existence. But our trip was without drugs, a journey carefully planned while we were both students and which became a solid reality.

"Reacting against the unquestioning belief in science that infected my parents' generation, Liv and I resolved to go 'back to nature', and chose as our paradise the Pacific island of Fatu-Hiva at the southern end of the Marquesas archipelago.

"Mountainous and remote, Fatu-Hiva had abundant fruit and drinking water, and—

Above If this is life *with* government, would things be better or worse *without*?

although it was a French colony—no white men. . . .

"And then the rains came. Not as a sudden deluge that carried away our cabin, but as a sneaking thief who stole the sun and left us in wet misery. Not a drop came through the thatched roof, but dampness penetrated everywhere and everything. The crisp banana leaves of our mattress lost their springiness, and a smell of mould began to transcend the aroma of spice and flower. Day and night our ears were filled with the sound of water: water that dripped, dropped, dribbled, splashed, sputtered, gushed, and streamed everywhere. Our cabin was a boat in a sea of mud.

"Gradually we were forced to restrict our movements to the area around our cabin because ugly boils and open wounds appeared on our feet. Liv had three boils as large as tea cups growing on her legs, while I had open wounds on my feet and ankles. Her painful boils expanded from inside without visible reason until they burst, whereas my wounds had begun as almost unnoticeable grazes.

"For days on end only hunger forced us out of our bamboo cabin, since we spent most of our time striving to keep our feet clean and dry, while washing our wounds with boiling water. We had no medicine of any kind, though on Tahiti we had been advised to bring ointment along as a cure for tropical boils. But we would have none of modern man's inventions. We had left behind all blessings and benefits of civilization together with what we considered its evils.

"We had come to Fatu-Hiva full of contempt for twentieth-century civilization, convinced that man had to start all over again from scratch. We had come to take a critical look at the modern world from the outside. Now we were sitting in our cave with a rock wall behind us, staring into the empty blue, waiting for the means to turn back, not to nature, but to civilization. We were milder in our judgement. We had seen that the mosquitoes could have driven us out of our minds in Fatu-Hiva's jungle, and infected us with elephantiasis; without medical treatment on Hivaoa, we might have ended up with no legs at all.

"Once we had admitted to ourselves and to each other that we wanted to return to our own world, we sat until dusk, eating clams and discussing civilization the way we saw it from a distance, with all its blessings and all its drawbacks. . . .

"We hated going back to civilization. But it was something we could not resist. We had to do it. We were sure then, and I still am, that the only place where it is possible to find nature is within yourself. There it is, unchanged, now as always." (Thor Heyerdahl, in the *Observer*.)

Some people believe that any form of government is undesirable, and that all forms of authority should be rejected. Anarchists question the right of authority to rule and believe that individuals should be free to do as they like without the constrictions of laws, constitutions and governments.

"To be governed is to be watched over, inspected, spied on, directed, legislated at, regulated, docketed, indoctrinated, preached at, controlled, assessed, weighed, censored, ordered about, by men who have neither the right nor the virtue. To be governed means to be, at each operation, at each transaction, at each movement, noted, registered, controlled, taxed, stamped, measured, valued, assessed, patented, licensed, authorized, endorsed, admonished, hampered, reformed, rebuked, arrested. It is to be, on the pretext of the general interest, taxed, drilled, held to ransom, exploited, monopolized, extorted, squeezed, hoaxed, robbed; then at the least resistance, at the first word of complaint, to be repressed, fined, abused, annoyed, followed, bullied, beaten, disarmed, garotted, imprisoned, machine-gunned, judged, condemned, deported, flayed, sold, betrayed and finally mocked, ridiculed, insulted, dishonoured. That's government, that's its justice, that's its morality." (P A Proudhoun in 1858, quoted in James Joll, *The Anarchists*.)

"The anarchists conceive of society in which all the mutual relations of its members are regulated, not by laws, not by authorities, whether self-imposed or elected, but by mutual agreements between the members of that society and by a sum of social customs and habits . . . continuously developing and continually readjusted in accordance with the ever-growing requirements of a free life. . . . No ruling authorities, then. No government of man by man . . . but a continual evolution such as we see in nature." (J P Kropotkin in *The Anarchists*.)

1. Clemenceau, who was a prime minister of France in the early 1900s, said: "I am sorry for anyone who has not been an anarchist at twenty." Why do you think he said this? Do you agree?

2. Would you like to have lived in the community that Robert Owen described?

3. Can you escape from the society into which you are born and brought up? What drove Thor Heyerdahl back to civilization?

4. What would be the attractions of leaving civilization behind? What would be the disadvantages?

5. Write a reply to Proudhoun's tirade on what government is, stating the good things about it.

Glossary

Act A law passed by Parliament.

Bill A proposed act, before it is passed by Parliament.

Cabinet The decision-making body of the Government. The Cabinet, which comprises the most senior ministers, makes policy decisions on home and foreign affairs, deals with unforeseen major problems and co-ordinates the policies of the different government departments.

Dissolution of Parliament The end of a parliament. Parliament can run its full five-year term, or it can be dissolved earlier by the Queen on the Prime Minister's advice. Often it is terminated when the Government feels confident of winning a general election, or because the Government has been defeated on a major issue.

Division When the House of Commons divides into party lobbies to vote on issues.

Electorate Collectively, the people who are eligible to vote.

Ombudsman The Parliamentary Commissioner for Administration. He investigates complaints into maladministration by government departments.

Order Paper The House of Commons agenda for each day.

Pressure groups Groups which try to influence government and public opinion to protect their special interests or to advance their beliefs, e.g. RSPCA, CBI, trade unions.

Private members Also known as backbenchers. Ordinary MPs without ministerial responsibilities.

Proportional Representation Electoral systems which reflect in a parliament the varying strengths of political parties. The commonest system is the transferable vote. Each constituency has several members. The most popular candidates are elected and the remaining seats distributed among the other candidates according to the voters' second and later choices.

Royal Assent A formal procedure in the House of Lords marking the final stage of a bill's progress. The Lords Commissioners represent the Queen, who is not present. After the title of a bill has been read to them, the Clerk of the Parliament gives the Royal Assent and the bill becomes law.

Further Reading

Alan Bullock, *Hitler: A Study in Tyranny,* Penguin, 1969.

Richard Crossman, *Inside View*, Cape, 1972.

Anthony King (ed), *Why is Britain Becoming Harder to Govern?*, BBC, 1976.

Lionel Kochan, *The Russian Revolution*, Wayland, 1971.

Peter Lane, *The Conservative Party*, Batsford, 1974.

Peter Lane, *The Labour Party*, Batsford, 1974.

Peter Lane, *The Liberal Party*, Batsford, 1974.

Peter Lane, *Political Parties*, Batsford, 1972.

Douglas Liversidge, *The House of Commons: The Lawmakers*, Franklin Watts, 1974.

Douglas Liversidge, *The House of Lords*, Franklin Watts, 1976.

Joe McGinniss, *The Selling of the President,* Deutsch, 1970.

William Morris, *News from Nowhere*, Routledge, 1970.

Robert Owen, *A New View of Society*, Dent, 1973.

Michael D Palmer, *Government*, Batsford, 1970.

Patrick J Rooke, *Parliament*, Wayland, 1970.

Richard Rose, *Politics in England Today*, Faber, 1974.

Bertrand Russell, *Has Man a Future?* Penguin, 1970.

Katharine Savage, *A History of the Common Market*, Longman, 1969.

Index

Acknowledgements

The author and publishers would like to thank the following for permission to reproduce illustrations on the pages listed:
Central Office of Information, Crown Copyright *frontispiece*, p 20, p 23, pp 42-43, p 68 (top), p 81; Conservative Party p 14; East Sussex County Council pp 34-35, p 36, p 68 (bottom); Henry Grant Photos p 7, p 19, p 54; Keystone Press Agency pp 8-9, p 11, p 12, pp 16-17, pp 24-25, p 26, p 29, p 31, p 32, p 41 (bottom), p 45 (bottom), p 47, pp 48-49, pp 50-51, pp 56-57, p 59, p 65, p 67, p 72, p 75, pp 76-77, pp 78-79, p 83, pp 86-87, pp 90-91; Liberal Party p 71; Mary Evans Picture Library p 89 (top and bottom); Metropolitan Police p 39; Popperfoto p 41 (top), p 45 (top); the remaining illustrations are the property of the Wayland Picture Library.